Series/Number 07-157

D0140076

LATENT GROWTH CURVE MODELING

Kristopher J. Preacher
University of Kansas

Aaron L. Wichman
Ohio State University

Robert C. MacCallum
University of North Carolina at Chapel Hill

Nancy E. Briggs
University of Adelaide

 SAGE

Los Angeles ■ London ■ New Delhi ■ Singapore

Copyright © 2008 by Sage Publications, Inc.

All rights reserved. No part of this book may be reproduced or utilized in any form or by any means, electronic or mechanical, including photocopying, recording, or by any information storage and retrieval system, without permission in writing from the publisher.

For information:

Sage Publications, Inc.
2455 Teller Road
Thousand Oaks, California 91320
E-mail: order@sagepub.com

Sage Publications India Pvt. Ltd.
B 1/I 1 Mohan Cooperative
    Industrial Area
Mathura Road, New Delhi 110 044
India

Sage Publications Ltd.
1 Oliver's Yard
55 City Road
London EC1Y 1SP
United Kingdom

Sage Publications
    Asia-Pacific Pte. Ltd.
33 Pekin Street #02-01
Far East Square
Singapore 048763

Printed in the United States of America

Library of Congress Cataloging-in-Publication Data

Latent growth curve modeling/Kristopher J. Preacher . . . [et al.].
    p. cm.—(Quantitative applications in the social sciences; 157)
Includes bibliographical references and index.
ISBN 978-1-4129-3955-3 (pbk.)

1. Latent structure analysis. 2. Latent variables. 3. Longitudinal method.
4. Social sciences—Statistical methods. I. Preacher, Kristopher J. II. Series.

QA278.6.L32 2008
519.5'35—dc22   2008006240

This book is printed on acid-free paper.

08   09   10   11   12   10   9   8   7   6   5   4   3   2   1

Acquisitions Editor:	Vicki Knight
Associate Editor:	Sean Connelly
Editorial Assistant:	Lauren Habib
Production Editor:	Cassandra Margaret Seibel
Copy Editor:	QuADS Prepress (P) Ltd.
Typesetter:	C&M Digitals (P) Ltd.
Proofreader:	Wendy Jo Dymond
Cover Designer:	Candice Harman
Marketing Manager:	Stephanie Adams

QA
278.6
·L32
2008

CONTENTS

About the Authors vii

Series Editor's Introduction viii

Acknowledgments x

1. Introduction 1
Overview of the Book 3
Latent Growth Curve Modeling:
 A Brief History and Overview 4
Model Specification and Parameter Interpretation 5
The Scaling of Time 10
Asynchronous Measurement 13
Assumptions 14
Parameter Estimation and Missing Data 15
Model Evaluation and Selection 18
Statistical Power 20

2. Applying LGM to Empirical Data 22
Data 22
Software 23
Overview of Model-Fitting Strategy 24
Model 0: The Null Model 25
Model 1: Random Intercept 26
Model 2: Fixed Intercept, Fixed Slope 28
Model 3: Random Intercept, Fixed Slope 30
Model 4: Random Intercept, Random Slope 31
Model 5: Multiple-Groups Analysis 34
Model 6: The Conditional Growth Curve Model 35
Model 7: Parallel Process Model 38
Model 8: Cohort-Sequential Designs 42
Model 9: Time-Varying Covariates 46
Model 10: Polynomial Growth Curves 50
Model 11: Unspecified Trajectories 52
Summary 53

3. Specialized Extensions   **57**
Growth Mixture Models   57
Piecewise Growth   59
Modeling Change in Latent Variables
     With Multiple Indicators   61
Structured Latent Curves   62
Autoregressive Latent Trajectory Models   66
Categorical and Ordinal Outcomes   66
Modeling Causal Effects Among Aspects of Change   68
Summary   70

4. Relationships Between LGM and Multilevel Modeling   **71**
MLM for Repeated-Measures Data   71
Model Specification   73
Parameter Estimation   74
Model Evaluation   75
Areas of Overlap Between MLM and LGM   75
Areas of Differentiation Between MLM and LGM   77
Software   79

5. Summary   **80**

Appendix   **82**
References   **84**
Index   **94**

ABOUT THE AUTHORS

Kristopher J. Preacher, PhD, is an assistant professor of quantitative psychology at the University of Kansas. His research focuses primarily on the use of factor analysis, structural equation modeling, and multilevel modeling to analyze longitudinal and correlational data. Other interests include developing techniques to test mediation and moderation hypotheses, bridging the gap between theory and practice, and studying model evaluation and model selection in the application of multivariate methods to social science questions.

Aaron L. Wichman is a postdoctoral teaching fellow in the social psychology program at Ohio State University. His research interests focus on social cognition and on the application of quantitative techniques to individual differences research, including personality assessment.

Robert C. MacCallum, PhD, has had a long and distinguished career as a respected quantitative psychologist. His primary research interests involve the study of quantitative models and methods for the analysis of correlational data, especially factor analysis, structural equation modeling, and multilevel modeling. Of particular interest is the use of such methods for the analysis of longitudinal data, with a focus on individual differences in patterns of change over time. He teaches courses in factor analysis and introductory and advanced structural equation modeling. He currently serves as the director of the L. L. Thurstone Psychometric Laboratory at the University of North Carolina at Chapel Hill. He also holds the rank of Professor Emeritus from Ohio State University.

Nancy E. Briggs, PhD, is a statistician in the discipline of public health at the University of Adelaide. She serves primarily as a data analyst in various research projects in the health and behavioral sciences. Her research and professional interests involve the application of advanced multivariate statistical techniques, such as linear and nonlinear multilevel models and latent variable models, to empirical data.

SERIES EDITOR'S INTRODUCTION

Consider a consistent finding produced by social science research in the past 25 years: Marriage increases happiness. Reviewing the literature on the topic, Stack and Eshleman (1998) summarized that "[t]he advantage of the married over those who are not married appears to hold true for a specific indicator of well-being—global happiness" (p. 527). Studying data from 17 nations, they concluded that "marriage increases happiness equally among men and women" (p. 527). At issue are two questions—whether marriage increases happiness and whether the increase is equal between the sexes (or greater for men than women, as some argued). An additional question of interest is whether this incremental happiness, different or not between the sexes, changes over the life course of a marriage. Analyzing a national 17-year, 5-wave sample, VanLaningham, Johnson, and Amato (2001) found no support for the U-shaped pattern of marital happiness over the life course (a decline as well as an upturn of happiness in later years) as suggested by the literature.

There are two general methodological approaches to the research problem above: analyzing cross-sectional or longitudinal data by comparing those who are married with those who are not. Much of the research on the topic analyzes cross-sectional data. However, for a proper assessment of the simple statement that "marriage increases happiness," longitudinal data are a must. Some, like VanLaningham et al. (2001), do use a version of panel analytic models (in their case, the fixed-effects model). What we really mean to study is the following scenario: A random sample of unmarried individuals at Time 0 are followed-up, some of them get married at Time 1, some at Time 2, etc., and some remain unmarried for the entire observational period until the end of their life course (or the end of the observational period, whichever happens first). The cross-sectional approach takes a snapshot of the sample by comparing happiness between married and unmarried persons, thus ignoring unobserved individual heterogeneity. A panel analytic method (such as a fixed-effects, random-effects, or mixed-effects model) appropriately takes care of the problem of unobserved heterogeneity. Even more appropriate can be the method of latent growth curve models, with which the data analyst can not only deal with unobserved heterogeneity but also model the latent tendencies of happiness over the life course after marriage, separately for males and females.

Preacher, Wichman, MacCallum, and Briggs's *Latent Growth Curve Modeling* offers the readers of the *Quantitative Applications for the Social Sciences* series a unique chance to study a method that will be suitable for analyzing substantive problems like the one described above and to go beyond the empirical literature represented by what was discussed above. They show how a latent growth curve model is represented and estimated as a structural equation model and how it relates to a multilevel model, two methods that the series already covers (No. 34, *Covariance Structure Models: An Introduction to LISREL* by J. Scott Long, and No. 143, *Multilevel Modeling* by Douglas Luke). They show in the book various types of the model such as models of fixed/random intercepts and/or fixed/random slopes, the conditional growth curve model, the parallel process model, and multiple group analysis, and they discuss the extensions to the model such as piecewise growth, structured latent curves, and categorical and ordinal outcomes. Their presentations and discussions are accompanied by many illustrative figures, a benefit of using the structural equation model framework.

—*Tim Futing Liao*
Series Editor

ACKNOWLEDGMENTS

This work was funded in part by National Institute on Drug Abuse Grant DA16883 awarded to the first author while at the University of North Carolina at Chapel Hill. The authors wish to thank Sonya K. Sterba for her assistance in organizing the example applications, and to thank Gregory R. Hancock for providing thorough and thoughtful feedback on earlier drafts.

The authors also wish to acknowledge the NICHD Early Child Care Research Network for furnishing permission to use a portion of the NICHD Study of Early Child Care and Youth Development data set. The study is directed by a steering committee and supported by NICHD through a cooperative agreement (U10) that calls for a scientific collaboration between the grantees and NICHD staff.

LATENT GROWTH CURVE MODELING

Kristopher J. Preacher
University of Kansas

Aaron L. Wichman
Ohio State University

Robert C. MacCallum
University of North Carolina at Chapel Hill

Nancy E. Briggs
University of Adelaide

CHAPTER 1. INTRODUCTION

A fundamental observation in the social and behavioral sciences is that people change over time, but not necessarily in the same way or at the same rate. For example, verbal ability increases steadily throughout the elementary school years, but it does not increase at the same rate for all students. There are individual differences in the rate and direction of change in many contexts, and these individual differences in change are often of scientific or practical interest. Change over time can be measured in seconds, as in studies of cardiac reactivity, or in decades, as in life span development studies. Marital arguments, for example, may cause significant endocrinological change over the course of only a few minutes, but these changes can be quite different for husbands than for wives (Kiecolt-Glaser et al., 1997). Flora and Chassin (2005) examined growth in drug use among adolescents as a function of parent alcoholism, following participants over a number of years through young adulthood. Early approaches to investigating change were very limited in that (a) they focused exclusively either on group-level or on individual-level growth and (b) they addressed only two occasions of measurement, resulting in data too impoverished to allow examination of some of the most basic and interesting hypotheses about change over time.

More extensive data and more advanced statistical methods are often needed to enable scientists to discern and understand not only the shape and direction of change (*trajectory*) but also to identify the sources and consequences of change.

Longitudinal designs can yield valuable information about trends in psychological phenomena as well as individual differences in aspects of change over time. The richness of such data increases with the number of waves of data collection. Willett (1989) and Willett and Sayer (1994) discuss several advantages associated with longitudinal data drawn from multiple waves of data collection, relative to two-wave data: (a) the quality of research findings will be enhanced, (b) psychological theories may suggest appropriate functional forms for growth, (c) it is possible to test hypotheses about systematic interindividual differences in growth, (d) it is possible to associate features of growth with background characteristics, and (e) precision and reliability in growth measurement is a rapid monotonic increasing function of the number of waves. In short, longitudinal data not only enhance the statistical power of hypothesis tests but also enable researchers to test hypotheses they would be unable to address with cross-sectional or two-wave data.

Although many techniques have been developed to capitalize on these desirable features of longitudinal data, the focus of this book is on *latent growth curve modeling* (LGM). LGM represents a broad class of statistical methods that permit better hypothesis articulation, provide enhanced statistical power, and allow greater correspondence between the statistical model and the theory under investigation relative to competing methods. LGM permits straightforward examination of *intra*individual (within-person) change over time as well as *inter*individual (between-person) variability in intraindividual change. LGM is appealing not only because of its ability to model change but also because it allows investigation into the antecedents and consequents of change.

A selection of the kinds of questions the LGM framework can enable scientists to articulate and test include the following:

- What is the shape of the mean trend over time?
- Does the initial level predict rate of change?
- Do two or more groups differ in their trajectories?
- Does rate of change or degree of curvature in the mean trend predict key outcomes?
- What variables are systematically associated with change over time?
- Are theoretical hypotheses about the trajectory tenable given observed data?

- Does significant between-person variability exist in the shape of the trajectory?
- Is change over time in one variable related to change over time in another variable?

This list is by no means exhaustive. We now provide an overview of the rest of the book.

Overview of the Book

This book is intended for readers interested in studying change in phenomena over time. However, because LGM is an application of structural equation modeling (SEM), it is recommended that the reader have a basic working knowledge of SEM. It is important that researchers interested in LGM also be modestly familiar with topics such as multiple linear regression, the use of path diagrams to represent models, model identification issues, and the concept of fixed and free parameters. Useful introductory SEM texts include Kline (2004), Maruyama (1997), and Raykov and Marcoulides (2000). A more advanced treatment can be found in Bollen (1989).

We demonstrate the utility and flexibility of the LGM technique by beginning with a very basic model and building on this basic model with common extensions that permit deeper understanding of change processes and better articulated hypothesis tests. With each step, we apply the model to an existing data set to demonstrate how researchers can approach problems in practice. We demonstrate how to use LISREL (Jöreskog & Sörbom, 1996), Mx (Neale, Boker, Xie, & Maes, 2003), and Mplus (L. K. Muthén & Muthén, 1998–2006)—three popular SEM applications—to fit these models to data, although other user-friendly SEM packages could be used (e.g., EQS, AMOS). All results were identical (or nearly so) in LISREL and Mx. Syntax is provided on our Web site,[1] but most of the models we describe can be applied using virtually any SEM software package. In addition, we provide an extensive reference section so that interested readers will know where to go for more information. Thus, this book will bring researchers up to speed in LGM, but it also serves as a gateway to literature that explores these topics in greater depth.

We begin with a summary of research leading up to the development of LGM. We then describe the formal model specification, followed by sections on parameter estimation and model evaluation. Following this introductory material, we describe the data set we use throughout this book and the software used for analyses. The remainder of the book is devoted to descriptions of specific models likely to be encountered or used in practice. Beginning with a basic (null) model, we explore more complex growth curve models by gradually relaxing constraints on parameters and adding additional variables to the model. We then explore some interesting and common extensions to the basic LGM, including related growth curves (multiple growth processes modeled simultaneously), cohort-sequential designs, the addition of time-varying covariates, and more complicated growth functions. Following these examples, we discuss relationships between LGM and other techniques, including growth mixture modeling, piecewise growth curves, modeling change in latent variables, and the interface between multilevel (random coefficients) modeling and LGM.

Latent Growth Curve Modeling:
A Brief History and Overview

Historically, *growth curve models* (e.g., Potthoff & Roy, 1964) have been used to model longitudinal data in which repeated measurements are observed for some outcome variable at a number of occasions. The *latent* growth curve approach is rooted in the *exploratory factor analysis* (EFA) and *principal components analysis* (PCA) literature. Covariances among repeated measures can be modeled with EFA (Baker, 1954; Rao, 1958) or PCA (Tucker, 1958, 1966). Factors or components are then conceptualized as *aspects of change* or *chronometric* (as opposed to psychometric) *factors* (McArdle, 1989; McArdle & Epstein, 1987), and loadings may be interpreted as parameters representing the dependence of the repeated measures on these unobservable aspects of change. These aspects of change could include, for example, linear, quadratic, or S-shaped trends. These approaches have a number of problems for the study of change, however. One primary obstacle to using these approaches in practice is rotational indeterminacy—there is no clear rotation criterion that would select a loading pattern conforming to interpretable aspects of change (e.g., a set of polynomial curves). Although attempts have been made to develop rotation criteria that could be used to identify smooth functions (e.g., Arbuckle & Friendly, 1977; Tucker, 1966), none were completely satisfactory. An additional limitation of these methods was that they approached the problem of modeling change from the standpoint of estimating free loadings representing unknown functional trends (an exploratory approach) rather than testing the feasibility of a *particular* set of loadings (a confirmatory approach). The ability to test specific hypothesized trends is of great interest to substantive researchers.

Meredith and Tisak (1990) described *latent curve analysis* (LCA), an application of *confirmatory factor analysis* (CFA) that neatly sidesteps the rotational indeterminacy problem by allowing researchers to specify loadings reflecting specific hypothesized trends in repeated-measures data. This LCA approach is equivalent to what we call LGM. Because LGM is an application of CFA, which in turn is a special case of SEM, growth curve models can be imbedded in larger theoretical models. For readers interested in more details of the historical development of LGM, Bollen and Curran (2006) provide a thorough overview of its history.

Several advantages are associated with the use of LGM over competing methods, such as ANCOVA and multilevel modeling. LGM permits the investigation of interindividual differences in change over time and allows the researcher to investigate the antecedents and consequences of change. LGM provides group-level statistics such as mean growth rate and mean intercept, can test hypotheses about specific trajectories, and allows the incorporation of both time-varying and time-invariant covariates. LGM possesses all the advantages of SEM, including the ability to evaluate the adequacy of models using model fit indices and model selection criteria, the ability to account for measurement error by using latent repeated measures, and the ability to deal effectively with missing data. It is straightforward to compare growth across multiple groups or populations. LGM is a very flexible modeling strategy and can be easily adapted to new situations with unusual requirements.

Curran and Willoughby (2003) make an important point in stating that growth curve models "might be viewed as residing at an intersection between variable-centered and person-centered analysis" (p. 603). An exclusively variable-centered (nomothetic) perspective of change emphasizes mean trends over time, whereas an exclusively person-centered (idiographic) perspective focuses only on idiosyncratic trends characterizing individuals. Important insights can be gained from each perspective. Rather than focusing on one or the other, LGM capitalizes on both nomothetic aspects of change over time (mean trends) and idiographic aspects (individual departures from the mean trend).

Model Specification and Parameter Interpretation

A latent growth model can be represented as a special case of SEM. SEM is a general modeling framework for specifying and testing hypothesized patterns of relationships among sets of variables, some of which are measured (observed) while others are latent (unobserved). Latent variables often serve as proxies for psychological constructs that are impossible to measure directly. A typical structural equation model contains a small number of latent variables linked by path coefficients, which are interpreted as regression weights. Latent variables, in turn, are represented by measured indicator variables. The relationship between latent variables and indicators corresponds to the factor analysis model. That is, factor loadings represent effects of latent variables on their indicators.

A special case of this general SEM system yields the basic latent growth curve model. We present this special case here, and in subsequent developments involving more complex LGM, we employ more of the full SEM framework. In LGM, the measured variables are repeated measures of the same variable y. The latent variables of primary importance are not psychological constructs; they instead represent patterns, or aspects, of change in y. In a basic LGM, often two factors are specified to represent aspects of change. These factors are defined by specifying factor loadings of repeated measures of y such that the factor loadings describe trends over time in y. The *intercept factor* represents the level of the outcome measure, y, at which the time variable equals zero, and the *slope factor* represents the linear rate at which the outcome measure changes. For example, a researcher interested in the rate of linear change in children's externalizing could collect repeated measurements of externalizing behavior, then treat these repeated measurements as indicators of intercept and slope factors (constraining loadings to reflect the expected pattern of change in that variable). As we will illustrate, the flexibility of the LGM framework permits the specification of more sophisticated models as well.

An LGM can be represented in matrix notation in terms of a *data model*, a *covariance structure*, and a *mean structure*. The data model represents the relationship between the factors and the repeated measures of y.[2] This model represents the $p \times 1$ vector of observations ($\mathbf{y}$) as a linear function of intercepts ($\boldsymbol{\tau}_y$, $p \times 1$), m latent variables representing aspects of change ($\boldsymbol{\eta}$, $m \times 1$), and disturbance terms ($\boldsymbol{\varepsilon}$, $p \times 1$), treating factor loadings ($\boldsymbol{\Lambda}_y$, $p \times m$) as regression coefficients[3]:

$$\mathbf{y} = \boldsymbol{\tau}_y + \boldsymbol{\Lambda}_y \boldsymbol{\eta} + \boldsymbol{\varepsilon}. \qquad (1.1)$$

The $\boldsymbol{\tau}_y$ term is typically fixed to zero for model identification reasons. In expanded form (for $m = 2$), this model represents y_{ti}, the score at occasion t for individual i, as a function of two latent variables (η_{1i} and η_{2i}) and an error term (ε_{ti}):

$$y_{ti} = \lambda_{1t}\eta_{1i} + \lambda_{2t}\eta_{2i} + \varepsilon_{ti}. \qquad (1.2)$$

The latent variables, in turn, may be expressed as functions of latent means (α_1 and α_2) and individual deviations away from those means:

$$\eta_{1t} = \alpha_1 + \zeta_{1t}, \tag{1.3}$$

$$\eta_{2i} = \alpha_2 + \zeta_{2i}. \tag{1.4}$$

The latent variables η_{1i} and η_{2i} are often referred to as *random coefficients*. The ζ residuals, representing individuals' deviations from the means of η_{1i} and η_{2i}, are sometimes referred to as *random effects*.

From the data model in Equation 1.1, one can derive a covariance structure and a mean structure. The covariance structure represents the population variances and covariances of the repeated measures of y as functions of model parameters, and the mean structure represents the population means of those repeated measures as another function of model parameters. The mean and covariance structures differ from the data model in that they do not contain scores for individuals on the factors (e.g., intercept and slope factors). These models are often used for parameter estimation and model evaluation. In the covariance structure, the variances and covariances of observed variables (Σ, $p \times p$) are represented as functions of factor loadings (Λ_y), factor variances and covariances (Ψ, $m \times m$), and disturbance variances and covariances (Θ_ε, $p \times p$) (Bollen, 1989):

$$\Sigma = \Lambda_y \Psi \Lambda_y' + \Theta_\varepsilon. \tag{1.5}$$

The mean structure, obtained by taking the expectation of the data model, represents population means of observed variables (μ_y, $p \times 1$) as functions of intercepts (τ_y, $p \times 1$) and latent variable means (α, $m \times 1$):

$$\mu_y = \tau_y + \Lambda_y \alpha. \tag{1.6}$$

In LGM, the elements of τ_y are typically (but not always) constrained to zero, yielding a simplified data model and mean structure. Thus, the parameters of interest are contained in the matrices Λ_y, Ψ, and Θ_ε and the vector α. Columns of Λ_y are known as *basis curves* or *latent growth vectors* (Singer & Willett, 2003).

In the model in Figure 1.1, Y1 through Y5 represent equally spaced repeated measures of variable Y. Here, change in Y is modeled as a function of two basis curves, and thus, the loading matrix Λ_y has two columns. Loadings on the intercept factor are fixed to 1.0 to represent the influence of a constant on the repeated measures. Loadings on the slope factor are fixed to a linear progression to represent linearly increasing growth over time. Although it is traditional to begin the slope loadings at 0 to indicate that the first occasion of measurement indicates the initial response, this is by no means necessary, and indeed is often contraindicated. Additional factors are possible, each representing additional aspects of growth, often, but not necessarily, polynomial (see Model 10 in Chapter 2). In addition, the covariances among these aspects of change can be estimated by specifying covariance paths among factors. The ability to estimate these covariances can be important in situations where, for example, it is of interest to determine whether rate of growth in some variable is related to initial status. The triangle in Figure 1.1 represents the constant 1.0. Thus, the path coefficients linking the triangle to the basis factors are regressions onto a constant and, thus, represent means of the intercept and slope factors.

In the matrix representation of the covariance structure of Y1 through Y5, specifying the loadings of the repeated measures on intercept and slope factors equates to completely specifying the contents of Λ_y, the factor loading matrix. The important parameters, including the necessary constraints for a simple linear growth model with homoscedastic and uncorrelated disturbance variances, are

$$\Lambda_y = \begin{bmatrix} 1 & 0 \\ 1 & 1 \\ 1 & 2 \\ 1 & 3 \\ 1 & 4 \end{bmatrix}, \tag{1.7}$$

$$\Psi = \begin{bmatrix} \psi_{11} & \\ \psi_{21} & \psi_{22} \end{bmatrix}, \tag{1.8}$$

$$\alpha = \begin{bmatrix} \alpha_1 \\ \alpha_2 \end{bmatrix}, \tag{1.9}$$

$$\Theta_\varepsilon = \begin{bmatrix} \theta_\varepsilon & & & & \\ 0 & \theta_\varepsilon & & & \\ 0 & 0 & \theta_\varepsilon & & \\ 0 & 0 & 0 & \theta_\varepsilon & \\ 0 & 0 & 0 & 0 & \theta_\varepsilon \end{bmatrix}. \tag{1.10}$$

Interpretation of the parameters in these matrices is straightforward. Elements of Λ_y are fixed by the researcher to represent hypothesized trajectories, where each column of loadings represents a hypothesized aspect of change. In Equation 1.7, all elements in the first column are constrained to 1.0 to reflect the fact that each individual's intercept

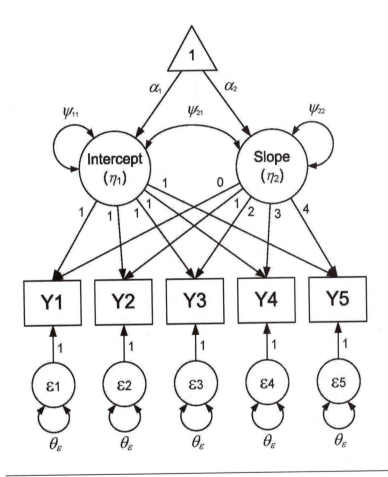

Figure 1.1   A Complete Path Diagram for a Typical Latent Growth Curve Model, Including Random Intercept, Random Linear Slope, and Intercept–Slope Covariance Parameters.

NOTE: By SEM convention, circles represent latent variables, squares represent measured variables (here, Y1 through Y5 are equally spaced repeated measures), triangles represent constants, double-headed arrows represent variances or covariances, and single-headed arrows represent regression weights. Numerical values correspond to fixed parameters, whereas symbols represent free parameters (those to be estimated).

remains constant over the repeated measures. The linear progression in the second column of Λ_y reflects the hypothesis of linear growth with equal time intervals. Elements of Ψ represent the variances and covariances of these aspects of change. In the case of simple linear growth represented in Figure 1.1, the Ψ matrix includes the intercept variance (ψ_{11}), the slope variance (ψ_{22}), and the covariance of intercepts and slopes (ψ_{21}). The elements of α are regression coefficients predicting aspects of change from a constant (1.0), and can be interpreted as the mean intercept and slope. In particular, α_2 in Equation 1.9 represents the expected change in the outcome variable associated with a change of one unit in the time metric. Finally, elements of Θ_ε are variances and covariances of disturbance terms, representing the portion of the variance in data not associated with the hypothesized latent curves.[4] If homoscedastic disturbance variance is assumed (as they are in Equation 1.10), the single disturbance variance may be represented by placing an equality constraint on the diagonal elements of Θ_ε. The off-diagonal terms in Θ_ε are usually fixed to zero to represent the hypothesis that disturbances are uncorrelated over time, although this assumption is not required. This basic LGM may be extended to incorporate predictors of intercept and/or slope, parallel growth curves for multiple outcomes, and parameter constraints (e.g., the covariance of the intercept and slope may be constrained to zero). These extensions and others are discussed later.

To summarize, there are six parameters estimated in a typical linear application of LGM, regardless of the number of repeated measurements. These include the mean intercept and slope (α_1 and α_2), the intercept and slope variances and covariance (ψ_{11}, ψ_{22}, and ψ_{21}), and a disturbance variance (θ_ε) that remains constant over repeated measurements. The remaining parameters are typically constrained to zero or to values consistent with a particular pattern of change. As you will see, some of these constraints can be changed or relaxed in various ways, depending on the characteristics of particular applications. Additional free parameters are added to the model in more complex models, such as those involving nonlinear growth or predictors of change over time.

The Scaling of Time

In Figure 1.1 and Equation 1.7, time was coded in a way that expressed linear change, placing the origin of the time scale at the first occasion of measurement ($\lambda_{1,2} = 0$). The loading pattern illustrated in Equation 1.7, in which the intercept is interpreted as "initial status," is typical, but other patterns may be useful as well, depending on the particular research question under consideration. Consider a case in which the last occasion of measurement (e.g., graduation from a drug rehabilitation program) is the occasion of most interest. In such situations, it is more sensible to code the final occasion of measurement as 0, as in the following loading matrix:

$$\Lambda_y = \begin{bmatrix} 1 & -4 \\ 1 & -3 \\ 1 & -2 \\ 1 & -1 \\ 1 & 0 \end{bmatrix}. \tag{1.11}$$

In Equation 1.11, the slope loadings increase linearly, but the intercept is defined to lie at the fifth, and last, occasion. In addition, if it is more sensible to code time in terms of months rather than years, Equation 1.11 could be reparameterized as follows:

$$\Lambda_y = \begin{bmatrix} 1 & 0 \\ 1 & 12 \\ 1 & 24 \\ 1 & 36 \\ 1 & 48 \end{bmatrix}. \tag{1.12}$$

The interpretation of some model parameters related to the slope factor (e.g., the mean slope or regression weights associated with predictors of slope) will be different for loading matrices in Equations 1.11 and 1.12, but the fit of the overall model will not. In fact, any linear transformation of the loading matrix will not alter model fit, although transformation of Λ_y does have important consequences for parameter interpretation (Biesanz, Deeb-Sossa, Papadakis, Bollen, & Curran, 2004; Hancock & Lawrence, 2006; Mehta & West, 2000; Rogosa & Willett, 1985; Stoel, 2003; Stoel & van den Wittenboer, 2003; Stoolmiller, 1995; Willett, Singer, & Martin, 1998). It is rarely sensible, for example, to center the time variable at its mean because the central occasion of measurement is not usually of most interest.[5] Rather, time should be coded in a way that facilitates answering substantive questions. The zero point of the time scale should be placed at a meaningful occasion of measurement, in part because this choice determines the point in time at which to interpret the mean intercept, intercept variance, and intercept–slope covariance (Rogosa & Willett, 1985). Stoel (2003) and Stoel and van den Wittenboer (2003) suggest that the intercept is meaningful only for growth processes with a natural origin; if the time origin is chosen arbitrarily, interpretation of any intercept-related parameters should be avoided. Similarly, the metric of time should be chosen so as to maximize interpretability (Biesanz et al., 2004). In some circumstances, this may involve using two metrics of time simultaneously in the same model (e.g., age and wave; see McArdle & Anderson, 1990).

A common question concerns the optimal number of repeated measures to use. To a large extent this choice will be dictated by practical concerns such as time and cost. The minimum number of repeated measures necessary to achieve a model with at least one degree of freedom (df) for m polynomial growth factors, regardless of whether or not the disturbance variances are constrained to equality over time, is $m + 1$. This formula will always hold, assuming that the estimated parameters include only factor means, factor (co)variances, and disturbance variances. A model with at least 1 df (i.e., an overidentified model) is necessary because, if there are at least as many free parameters as there are sample means and (co)variances, the model will not be identified and will thus be untestable (see Bollen, 1989; Bollen & Curran, 2006, for more details on model identification).

But how many repeated measures should be used, given $m + 1$ as an absolute minimum? Stoolmiller (1995) suggests that four to five measurement occasions are probably sufficient for modeling linear growth. MacCallum, Kim, Malarkey, and Kiecolt-Glaser (1997) note that there is no reliable rule of thumb, but suggest that linear models demand at least four or five repeated measures, whereas more complex models may demand "substantially more than that" (p. 217). To obtain adequate power for testing covariances among slope factors in parallel process latent growth curve models (Model 7 in Chapter 2), Hertzog, Lindenberger, Ghisletta, and von Oertzen (2006) recommend that at least six repeated measures be collected, but this figure may shift up or down with changes in effect size, sample size, or growth curve reliability (the ratio of total variance explained by aspects of growth). As in almost every other aspect of data analysis, more is better—more data yield more information, and that is never a bad thing. However, it is our experience that parsimonious linear models often have trouble adequately fitting more than six repeated measures. This should come as no surprise, as few natural processes are likely to follow precisely linear trajectories. *No model is correct*, so researchers should be prepared to see simple models fit poorly as information accumulates. LGM is best suited for modeling trends measured over a limited number of occasions in large samples. Regardless of the number of measurements, the *range* of measurement should be sufficient to span the entire time frame of theoretical interest.

Finally, we note that occasions of measurement need not be equally spaced. For example, if longitudinal data were collected in 1977, 1979, 1983, and 1984, the intervals between occasions of measurement become 2, 4, and 1:

$$\Lambda_y = \begin{bmatrix} 1 & 0 \\ 1 & 2 \\ 1 & 6 \\ 1 & 7 \end{bmatrix}. \tag{1.13}$$

The loading matrix in Equation 1.13 still represents linear change; the intervals between slope loadings are themselves linear rescalings of the intervals between occasions of measurement. If one takes 1977 as a baseline, subsequent measurement occasions occurred 2, 6, and 7 years after it. In nonlinear models (such as the polynomial latent curve models described in Chapter 2 or the structured latent curve models discussed in Chapter 3), it is often a good idea to not only collect more than five repeated measures but also to space measurements more closely together during periods when change is occurring the most rapidly. This helps avoid estimation problems and to more accurately estimate parameters characterizing change.

Our point is that there is no "one-size-fits-all" design and corresponding growth curve model. The number of measurement waves, times between waves, units of time, and placement of the time origin may vary greatly both within and across studies. More in-depth discussion of the scaling of time may be found in Biesanz et al. (2004), Curran and Willoughby (2003), Hancock and Choi (2006), Schaie (1986), and Stoolmiller (1995).

Asynchronous Measurement

Loadings in Λ_y are fundamentally unlike other fixed parameters with which users of SEM may be familiar. Regardless of how time is coded, the contents of Λ_y represent *functions of time*. For example, the slope loadings contain values of what might be considered the predictor *time* in other modeling contexts. Many applications of LGM make the oversimplifying assumption that data are collected at the same occasions across all individuals (Mehta & West, 2000). Such data are referred to as *time-structured data* (Bock, 1979). The fact that all subjects share the same occasions of measurement permits these values to be placed in a common Λ_y matrix. But this is unrealistic in most applications. In situations where individuals are not measured at the same occasions, or are measured at the same occasions but at different ages, the basic LGM described earlier will not be sufficient. As we now discuss, there are two main strategies for estimating growth curve models in situations when individuals are measured at different occasions. Both strategies allow for individual differences in factor loadings.

When all individuals are not measured at the same occasions, but there is a limited set of measurement schedules, a multiple-group strategy can be employed in which multiple models, each characterized by a distinct Λ_y matrix, are estimated simultaneously. We discuss this strategy in more detail in the next section, but basically it involves placing individuals with the same measurement schedule into groups and fitting the model simultaneously to all such groups (Allison, 1987; T. E. Duncan, Duncan, Strycker, Li, & Alpert, 1999; McArdle & Bell, 2000; McArdle & Hamagami, 1991; B. Muthén, Kaplan, & Hollis, 1987). Thus, all individuals measured only at times 1, 3, 5, and 6 may belong to Group 1, whereas all individuals measured only at times 1, 2, 4, and 5 may belong to Group 2.

But consider the case in which there are too many distinct measurement schedules to be accommodated by the multiple-groups solution. A more general solution exists. An attractive feature of the Mx and Mplus programs is that they can accommodate individual slope loadings via implementation of *definition variables*, or *individual data vectors*—special parameter vectors containing fixed values for each individual (Hamagami, 1997; Neale et al., 2003). Whereas the traditional approach involves applying a model in which all individuals are assumed to share the same basis curves and thus the same Λ_y, the use of definition variables involves creating a set of slope factor loadings unique to each individual. In the special case of longitudinal research involving age, this is referred to as *scaling age across individuals* (Mehta & West, 2000). A sample Mx script demonstrating this technique is included in Appendix A of Mehta and West (2000) and at our Web site (http://www.quantpsy.org/).

Assumptions

LGM with maximum likelihood (ML) estimation invokes certain important assumptions. Most assumptions involve the distributions of latent variables (in LGM, these are, for instance, intercept, slopes, and disturbances). Because these variables are by definition unobservable, it is customary to assume their characteristics. We assume that the means of residuals and disturbance terms in Equations 1.2, 1.3, and 1.4 are zero. At each occasion, this assumption applies to means computed across the population of individuals and across theoretical repeated observations of the same person. In other words, if it were possible to measure the same individual repeatedly at a given occasion, we assume that the mean of the disturbances across those measurements is zero. In a similar sense, the covariances among all residual terms are assumed to be zero within and between occasions, and all covariances between residuals in Equation 1.2 and random intercepts and slopes are assumed to be zero. To use ML estimation, it is necessary to make the additional assumption that observed variables are derived from population distributions with roughly the same multivariate kurtosis as a multivariate normal distribution. The assumptions underlying LGM are treated extensively by Bollen and Curran (2006).

Byrne and Crombie (2003) discuss three additional assumptions. They require the assumptions that the trajectory be linear, that the disturbances be uncorrelated across occasions, and that the disturbance variances remain equal across occasions. In fact, these are not assumptions of LGM or of ML. Byrne and Crombie's assumption of linearity refers to the linearity of the growth trajectory, not to the loadings. Technically, this is not an assumption; rather, it is the central hypothesis under scrutiny. Two ways to test the hypothesis of linearity are to compare the fit of a linear growth curve model to a baseline of absolute fit or relative to an unspecified trajectory model (see Model 11 in Chapter 2). The other two assumptions discussed by Byrne and Crombie (independence and homoscedasticity of disturbances) may be common aspects of model specification in LGM but are not required; in fact, the ability to estimate different occasion-specific disturbance variances is considered a strength of the LGM approach and is required for approaches that combine LGM with autoregressive strategies (Curran & Bollen, 2001; McArdle, 2001).

Parameter Estimation and Missing Data

Parameter estimation in SEM traditionally is accomplished with ML estimation, the use of which assumes that measured variables are multivariate normally distributed. For models such as latent growth curve models that are designed to explain covariances as well as means of measured variables, the data are typically in the form of a sample covariance matrix, S, and sample mean vector, $\bar{y}$, computed from complete data (the data are sometimes forced to be complete through listwise deletion or one of several data imputation methods). Matrix S is of order $p \times p$ and contains the sample variances and covariances of the p repeated measures of y. Vector $\bar{y}$ contains the sample means of those p repeated measures. According to the covariance and mean structure models in Equations 1.5 and 1.6, the population covariance matrix, Σ, and mean vector, μ, are functions of model parameters. If we let all the parameters in Equations 1.5 and 1.6 be organized into a single vector, θ, then the objective in parameter estimation is to find parameter estimates in $\hat{\theta}$ such that the resulting implied Σ and μ are as similar as possible to S and $\bar{y}$, respectively. In ML estimation, this optimality is defined using the multivariate normal likelihood function. That is, ML estimation results in a set of parameter estimates $\hat{\theta}$ that maximize the log of the likelihood function:

$$\ln L = -\frac{1}{2}\sum_{i=1}^{N}\left\{ p \ln 2\pi + \ln|\Sigma| + (\mathbf{y}_i - \mathbf{\mu})'\Sigma^{-1}(\mathbf{y}_i - \mathbf{\mu})\right\}. \quad (1.14)$$

Extending developments by Jöreskog (1967), it can be shown that $\ln L$ is maximized when the following *discrepancy function* is minimized:

$$F_{ML} = \ln|\Sigma| - \ln|S| + \text{tr}\left[(S - \Sigma)\Sigma^{-1}\right] + (\bar{\mathbf{y}} - \mathbf{\mu})'\Sigma^{-1}(\bar{\mathbf{y}} - \mathbf{\mu}). \quad (1.15)$$

Thus, given S and $\bar{y}$, ML estimation seeks a vector of parameter estimates, $\hat{\theta}$, that produce implied Σ and μ matrices (from Equations 1.5 and 1.6) that minimize F_{ML}. Note that if $\Sigma = S$ and $\mu = \bar{y}$—that is, if the model perfectly reproduces the data—then $F_{ML} = 0$.

The minimization of the F_{ML} discrepancy function assumes that complete sample data are used to obtain S and $\bar{y}$. If some data are missing—for example, if individuals are measured at different occasions or if data simply are not obtained for some individuals at some occasions—this strategy will not work because covariance matrices computed using the available data may not be internally consistent. Fortunately, options are available for dealing with missing data. The multiple-group strategy mentioned earlier in the context of multiple measurement schedules can be considered a general model-based approach to addressing missing data (T. E. Duncan & Duncan, 1995; Marini, Olsen, & Rubin, 1979; McArdle & Hamagami, 1992; B. Muthén et al., 1987). For example, if some individuals are measured at occasions 1, 2, 3, and 5 and others are measured at occasions 1, 3, 4, and 5, a two-group model may be specified in which all members within each group share the same occasions of measurement. For multisample analyses, the discrepancy function in Equation 1.15 is generalized to a multisample expression and is then minimized so that optimal fit is obtained to all groups simultaneously.

The multiple-groups approach to dealing with missing data becomes impractical when there are more than a few distinct measurement schedules. Until recently, this limitation presented a real problem, given the prevalence of missing data in real longitudinal designs. Advances in estimation that allow models to be fit directly to raw data have made it possible to include incomplete cases in the analysis. In situations involving missing (partially complete) data, the *full information maximum likelihood* (FIML) method is often recommended to obtain ML parameter estimates. To allow for incomplete data, the log likelihood in Equation 1.14, which implies the availability of complete data, can be modified as follows:

$$\ln L = -\frac{1}{2}\sum_{i=1}^{N}\left\{p_i \ln 2\pi + \ln|\mathbf{\Sigma}_i| + (\mathbf{y}_i - \mathbf{\mu}_i)'\mathbf{\Sigma}_i^{-1}(\mathbf{y}_i - \mathbf{\mu}_i)'\right\}, \qquad (1.16)$$

where $\mathbf{y}_i$ is the measured portion of the data vector for individual i and $\mathbf{\mu}_i$ and $\mathbf{\Sigma}_i$ are the modeled mean vector and covariance matrix, respectively, with rows and columns corresponding to the data present for individual i (Arbuckle, 1996; Wothke, 2000). FIML estimation involves maximizing this function. FIML is more efficient and less biased than methods involving data imputation or deletion of partial data and yields unbiased estimates when data are missing completely at random (MCAR) or *missing at random* (MAR; Neale, 2000; Rubin, 1976).[6] When compared with pairwise and listwise deletion and imputation methods, FIML has been shown to have a lower incidence of convergence failure, higher efficiency, lower bias, and more accurate model rejection rates (Enders & Bandalos, 2001). The characteristics of the two methods are similar. In fact, they are equivalent when no data are missing. For a clear, more in-depth description of the FIML algorithm with comparisons to other methods, see Enders (2001).

FIML is only one of several discrepancy functions that can be minimized to yield parameter estimates in the presence of missing data. Other approaches include the application of generalized least squares, unweighted least squares, the E-M algorithm, and asymptotically distribution free methods to data that have been rendered "complete" through pairwise or listwise deletion or through single or multiple imputation. FIML is often preferable to these methods because (a) it uses all available information to estimate parameters, (b) it does not require extremely large samples, and (c) standard errors may be obtained by inverting the asymptotic covariance matrix of parameter estimates. Pairwise and listwise deletion omit some data from consideration, and pairwise deletion risks the possibility of encountering a covariance matrix that is not positive definite. Furthermore, FIML is now a standard estimation option in most SEM software, including AMOS (Arbuckle & Wothke, 1999), Mplus (L. K. Muthén & Muthén, 1998–2006), Mx (Neale et al., 2003), EQS (Bentler, 1995), and LISREL

(Jöreskog & Sörbom, 1996). In LISREL, for example, FIML is automatically invoked if raw data are used as input. Missing data issues are discussed in more depth by Allison (1987, 2002). The primary drawback to using FIML estimation is that, if some data are missing, the full array of ML fit indices is not available.[7]

Model Evaluation and Selection

Specifying and testing models as representations of theoretical predictions is fundamental to the practice of modern empirical science. In developing a model to be fit to observed data, it is critical that the specified model accurately reflect the predictions or implications of a substantive theory of growth (Collins, 2006; Curran, 2000; Curran & Hussong, 2003; Curran & Willoughby, 2003). In addition, although the focus here is on model evaluation, it is usually preferable not to specify and evaluate models in isolation, but rather to compare competing, theoretically derived models.

Given a theoretically plausible model, hypotheses in LGM can be tested by assessing the statistical and practical significance of model parameters, including the means of the intercept and slope factors and the variances and covariances among aspects of change. An informal test of the significance of a parameter is conducted by dividing the point estimate by its standard error; if the ratio exceeds about 2.00 (1.96 in very large samples), the parameter estimate is said to be significantly different from zero at the .05 level. The determination of practical significance depends heavily on the context.

In SEM, the fit of an entire model also can be assessed. Indeed, good fit by global criteria is usually a prerequisite for interpreting parameter estimates.[8] Under multivariate normality and under the null hypothesis of perfect fit, $\hat{F}_{ML} \times (N - 1)$ is distributed as χ^2 with degrees of freedom $df = [p(p + 3)/2] - q^*$, where p is the number of variables and q^* is the effective number of free model parameters.[9] This χ^2 statistic forms the basis for an array of fit indices that can be used to gauge the match between a model's predictions and observed data. We recommend the *root mean square error of approximation* (RMSEA; Browne & Cudeck, 1993; Steiger & Lind, 1980):

$$\text{RMSEA} = \sqrt{\frac{\max\left\{\left(\hat{F}_{ML} - \frac{df}{N-1}\right), 0\right\}}{df}}, \qquad (1.17)$$

available in several SEM programs. The numerator under the radical in Equation 1.17 is an estimate of model misfit (discrepancy) in the population. Thus, the quantity under the radical represents estimated population model error per degree of freedom and thus smaller values are better. RMSEA is preferred because it is an estimate of misfit in the population rather than simply a measure of misfit in the sample. Importantly, one can obtain confidence intervals for RMSEA, providing a measure of precision of this fit index in addition to a point value.

Because χ^2-based indices are known to suffer from problems associated with near-singular matrices (Browne, MacCallum, Kim, Andersen, & Glaser, 2002), violations of distributional assumptions (Curran, West, & Finch, 1996), and large N (Tucker & Lewis, 1973), it is also advisable to examine simple residuals between elements of $\mathbf{S}$ and $\hat{\mathbf{\Sigma}}$. A common index based only on residuals is the *standardized root mean square residual* (SRMR; Jöreskog & Sörbom, 1996), a summary measure of the magnitude of the residuals. SRMR is the square root of the average squared absolute difference between observed correlations and model-implied correlations (and thus smaller values are better). Like RMSEA, SRMR is included as default output in many SEM programs, although it should be kept in mind that SRMR assesses fit of the covariance structure only and is not sensitive to misfit in the mean structure.

Another family of fit indices reflects the *incremental fit* of the specified model over the fit of an appropriately specified null model (see Model 0 in Chapter 2). One example of this sort of fit index is the *nonnormed fit index* (NNFI; Bentler & Bonett, 1980; Tucker & Lewis, 1973):

$$\text{NNFI} = \min\left\{ \left(\frac{\frac{\chi_0^2}{df_0} - \frac{\chi_k^2}{df_k}}{\frac{\chi_0^2}{df_0} - 1} \right), 1 \right\}, \tag{1.18}$$

where χ_0^2 and df_0 are computed with respect to the null model, and χ_k^2 and df_k are computed with respect to the model of interest. NNFI has been demonstrated to be relatively robust to violations of distributional assumptions (Lei & Lomax, 2005). We elaborate on the appropriate null model in the next chapter. In this book, we report χ^2, RMSEA, NNFI, and SRMR for all fitted models.

In addition to evaluation of models in isolation, a model selection approach can be used to evaluate the relative fit of nested or nonnested models. One model is said to be nested in another if the estimated parameters of one (Model A) are a subset of those in the latter (Model B). In other words, if some of the parameters in B are constrained to yield A, A is nested within B. When some data are partially missing, some fit indices can no longer be computed (Enders, 2001), for example, GFI and SRMR.

Under the null hypothesis of no difference between models, the difference in χ^2 statistics ($\Delta\chi^2$) for complete data, or between $-2\ln L$ values for incomplete data, is itself distributed as a χ^2 statistic, with df equal to the difference in the number of parameters estimated. For models that are not nested, information-based model selection criteria (e.g., Akaike information criterion, Bayesian information criterion) may be used to select models.

Statistical Power

As with most applications of inferential statistics, statistical power is important in the LGM context. Power refers to the probability of correctly rejecting a false null hypothesis. In the LGM context, the null hypothesis is the researcher's latent growth curve model, so power is the probability that one's model of growth will be rejected if it is not correct in the population. LGM models are generally never exactly correct in the population, so a high level of statistical power will tend to ensure rejection of models that are very good, but not perfect. This rejection of good models is, of course, not desirable in practice, but is a well-known limitation of the likelihood ratio test of model fit. In practice, this situation is remedied through the use of various descriptive measures of fit such as those described earlier rather than focusing exclusively or heavily on the likelihood ratio test of model fit.

MacCallum, Browne, and Sugawara (1996) describe a method of computing power (given sample size) or minimum required sample size (given a desired level of power) that involves the RMSEA fit index. The researcher chooses null and alternative hypotheses corresponding to values of RMSEA that reflect, respectively, good fit (ε_0) and poor fit (ε_A). For example, the *test of exact fit* might involve selecting $\varepsilon_0 = 0.00$ (exact fit) and $\varepsilon_A = 0.08$ (mediocre fit). A test of close fit might involve selecting $\varepsilon_0 = 0.05$ (close fit) and $\varepsilon_A = 0.10$ (unacceptable fit). SAS code provided by the authors will supply the minimum N necessary for rejecting a poor model at a given level of power, model df, and a pair of null and alternative hypotheses defining good and poor fits in terms of RMSEA. Conversely, their code will supply the level of statistical power associated with a pair of null and alternative hypotheses given a particular N and model df.

In addition to the power to reject a poor model, it is also sensible to consider the power to detect nonzero parameters. This kind of power represents a largely unstudied topic in the LGM context. An exception is a recent study by Hertzog et al. (2006), who found that the power to detect slope covariances in parallel process latent growth curve models (see Model 7 in Chapter 2) depends heavily on effect size, the number of repeated measures, growth curve reliability, and sample size.

Notes

1. http://www.quantpsy.org/

2. For those readers familiar with the LISREL framework for model specification in SEM, the mathematical representation here uses the "all-y" model, where all latent variables are considered as endogenous.

3. Vectors are denoted by underscores, and matrices are denoted by boldface.

4. It is important to remember that elements of Θ_ε do not represent error variance in the usual sense. Rather, the tth variance in Θ_ε reflects the degree to which a linear model does not adequately capture individuals' scores at occasion t. Much of this variability may be due to error, but it also may be amenable to prediction by other variables.

5. Stoolmiller (1995), on the other hand, recommends centering the time variable in polynomial models to avoid estimation problems due to linear dependence among the polynomial terms.

6. Missing data (for x) are MCAR when "missingness" depends neither on observed nor unobserved responses of x or any other variable. Missing x data are MAR when missingness depends neither on observed nor unobserved responses of x after controlling for other variables in the data set (Allison, 2002).

7. Mplus is the only SEM software, of which we are aware, that will compute fit indices when some data are missing.

8. Perhaps owing to their highly constrained nature, it is common for growth curve models to fit poorly by global fit criteria. However, models may fit poorly in situations even when individual growth curves are approximated well. Coffman and Millsap (2006) recommend that global fit indices be supplemented with individual fit criteria.

9. This formulation of df assumes that sample data comprise both means and covariances. Growth curve models are almost always fit to means and covariances. If the mean structure is not modeled, $df = [p(p + 1)/2] - q^*$.

CHAPTER 2. APPLYING
LGM TO EMPIRICAL DATA

Data

In the following, we demonstrate how to use growth curve models in practice. For this demonstration, we use data from the National Institute of Child Health and Human Development (NICHD) Study of Early Child Care and Youth Development (NICHD Early Child Care Research Network, 2006). Quantification and subsequent analysis of parent–child relationships offer a relatively objective way to approach familial problems. A great deal of research examines the linkages between these relationships and outcomes such as smoking or drinking (e.g., Blackson, Tarter, Loeber, Ammerman, & Windle, 1996), self-regulation ability (e.g., Wills et al., 2001), and adolescent pregnancy (see Miller, Benson, & Galbraith, 2001, for a review). Good parent–child relationships are consistently found to be associated with positive child outcomes, but the associations between parent–child relationships at any given time and later outcome measures are typically moderate in size. One of the many reasons for the lack of perfect predictive validity of parent–child relationships is that these relationships change over time. Theoretical approaches ranging from the psychodynamic (e.g., Freud, 1958) to evolutionary (e.g., Steinberg, 1989) and social-cognitive (e.g., Smetana, 1988) all predict change in parent–child relationships as children mature, albeit for different reasons. Studying change over time in parent–child relationships provides additional opportunities to increase predictive accuracy, as well as to arrive at a more complete understanding of how parent–child interactions influence children's and adolescents' undesirable behaviors.

We selected two composite measures from the Child–Parent Relationship Scale. Specifically, 15 rating-scale items from the Student–Teacher Relationship Scale (Pianta, 1993) were adapted to assess parents' report of the child's attachment to the parent. Each item was scored on a scale of 1 to 5, where 1 = *Definitely does not apply* and 5 = *Definitely applies*. These items were used to construct four composite measures, labeled Conflict With Child (CNFL) and Closeness With Child (CLSN) for mothers and for fathers. These variables were assessed during the elementary school years, Grades 1 through 6 (data were not collected in the second grade). Mothers' Closeness to Child served as the primary repeated-measures variable for most of the models to be illustrated. In conjunction with these relationship measures, a grouping variable (child gender) was selected so that we could demonstrate how groups can be included in longitudinal models. We extracted data for all children who had at least one valid CLSN score, yielding a total sample size of 1,127 children (571 boys and 556 girls). Analyses were performed on all cases with complete data on the variables of interest.[1] Descriptive information is included in Table 2.1. Mean scores for CLSN are presented in Figure 2.1. Finally, the observed covariance matrix and means for the 851 complete-data cases in our sample are given in Table 2.2.

Software

The models described below were estimated using three software packages. We used LISREL 8.8 (Jöreskog & Sörbom, 1996), Mx 1.1 (Neale et al., 2003), and Mplus 4.2 (L. K. Muthén & Muthén, 1998–2006). Other user-friendly packages are available for analyzing growth curve models, such as AMOS and EQS. Mx is especially useful for its flexibility and the fact that it is public domain software, freely available for downloading. A free student version of LISREL, capable of estimating all models in this book, is available at the SSI Web site as of this writing.[2] Ferrer, Hamagami, and McArdle (2004) provide a guide to specifying growth curve models in a variety of software applications.

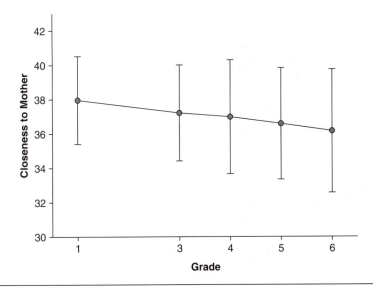

Figure 2.1   Mean Closeness Scores (Mothers), Grades 1–6. Error Bars Represent One Standard Deviation.

TABLE 2.1
Descriptive Statistics for Mother's Closeness to Child Data

	Entire Sample			Boys			Girls		
Grade	N	Mean	SD	N	Mean	SD	N	Mean	SD
Cases with incomplete data									
1	1,016	37.96	2.56	508	37.73	2.77	508	38.20	2.30
3	1,025	37.19	2.82	508	37.07	2.73	517	37.32	2.90
4	1,022	36.96	3.33	516	36.62	3.53	506	37.31	3.08
5	1,018	36.56	3.25	506	36.65	3.34	512	36.77	3.16
6	1,024	36.18	3.56	512	35.93	3.63	512	36.42	3.47
Cases with complete data									
1	851	37.95	2.53	417	37.76	2.66	434	38.14	2.38
3	851	37.28	2.74	417	37.20	2.62	434	37.35	2.86
4	851	37.05	3.28	417	36.74	3.45	434	37.34	3.07
5	851	36.57	3.21	417	36.34	3.31	434	36.79	3.09
6	851	36.14	3.59	417	35.84	3.73	434	36.42	3.43

TABLE 2.2
Mother–Child Closeness:
Means and Covariances of Cases With Complete Data ($N = 851$)

Grade	Means	Covariances				
1	37.9542	6.3944				
3	37.2785	3.2716	7.5282			
4	37.0463	4.1435	6.0804	10.7290		
5	36.5696	3.7058	5.1597	6.5672	10.2920	
6	36.1363	4.1286	5.7608	7.2365	7.6463	12.9085

Overview of Model-Fitting Strategy

A typical application of LGM to a problem with repeated measures contains variables measured at two levels of analysis. *Level 2 units* are the entities under study, which are usually (but not necessarily) individuals. *Level 1 units* are the repeated measurements taken on each Level 2 unit. Other variables may be measured either at Level 1 or at Level 2. Level 1 variables include the outcome (y) variable(s) and all other variables that are measured at the same occasion. Variables that are measured repeatedly and used to predict variability across repeated measures of the outcome are referred to as *time-varying covariates* (TVCs). Level 2 variables represent characteristics of the Level 2 units and thus vary *across* individuals rather than *within* individuals over time; examples might include gender, contextual variables, or stable personality traits. Level 2 predictors are often called *time-invariant covariates*. Variability in the intercept or slope factors may be explained by time-invariant covariates. For example, a researcher may be interested in the change in parents' perceptions of parent–child closeness as children age. She or he may collect data from the same parents on a number of occasions and may want to model the change in closeness over time. For this model, the researcher might choose the zero point of the time scale to lie at the first measurement occasion and then collect four subsequent waves of data from the same children. If the researcher finds that trajectories (intercepts and slopes) vary significantly across children, she or he may want to investigate whether gender differences explain some of that interindividual variability. Therefore, the researcher may introduce gender as a predictor of initial level (the intercept factor), of rate of change (the slope factor), or both. Here, gender is a time-invariant covariate because it varies over the Level 2 units (children) but not within Level 2 units.

Especially with a technique as flexible as LGM, it is helpful to specify a theoretically informed sequence of models to test before attempting to fit models to data. One then checks the fit of an a priori sequence of theoretically plausible models in the specified order. When models of increasing complexity no longer result in significant improvements in fit, one concludes than an acceptable model has been found. In the next section, we demonstrate this approach.

Model 0: The Null Model

The phrase *null model* generally is used to refer to a basis for comparison of hypothesized models. The null model in LGM is different from that in typical applications of SEM. In typical SEM applications, the null model is one in which no relationships are predicted among measured variables. Only variance parameters are estimated, and there are no latent variables. However, in the context of LGM, we define the null model to be a model in which there is no change over time and no overall variability in mean level (Widaman & Thompson, 2003). Only the mean level (intercept; α_1) and a common disturbance variance (θ_ε) are estimated:

$$\Lambda_y = \begin{bmatrix} 1 \\ \vdots \\ \vdots \\ \vdots \\ 1 \end{bmatrix}, \qquad (2.1)$$

$$\Psi = [0], \qquad (2.2)$$

$$\alpha = [\alpha_1], \qquad (2.3)$$

$$\Theta_\varepsilon = \begin{bmatrix} \theta_\varepsilon & & & \\ 0 & \ddots & & \\ & & \ddots & \\ 0 & & 0 & \theta_\varepsilon \end{bmatrix}, \qquad (2.4)$$

where Λ_y is a 5×1 matrix representing the fixed loadings of each of our 5 occasions of measurement on the intercept factor. In this model, there is hypothesized to be no change over time, so the slope factor is omitted altogether. Matrix Ψ is a 1×1 matrix containing the variance of the intercept, which is fixed to zero in this model. Θ_ε is a 5×5 diagonal matrix with all elements on the diagonal constrained to equality. This equality constraint represents the assumption of homoscedasticity.[3] Finally, α is a 1×1 matrix containing the estimated population mean, α_1. If it is determined that the null model is inappropriate for the data (it usually will be), the intercept variance is usually estimated and a linear slope factor included to represent change over time. Predictors of intercept and slope can be included, following either an a priori theory-guided approach or a more exploratory approach. This simple two-parameter model, or a model adhering as closely as possible to it, will serve as the null model throughout the rest of this chapter for purposes of computing NNFI.

Model 1: Random Intercept

The random intercept model is the simplest example of a latent growth curve model. In LGM, the random intercept model is equivalent to a one-factor CFA model incorporating a mean structure, with all factor loadings fixed to 1.0 and all disturbance variances constrained to equality (see Figure 2.2). The parameter matrices are specified as in Equations 2.1, 2.2, 2.3, and 2.4, save that $\Psi = [\psi_{11}]$, which corresponds to interindividual variability in overall level.

When we fit Model 1 to the data in Table 2.2 using LISREL, we obtained the parameter estimates reported in Table 2.3.[4] Results showed that there was significant unexplained intraindividual variance ($\hat{\theta}_\varepsilon$) and interindividual variance ($\hat{\psi}_{11}$). In both cases, the significance of these parameters is seen by their size relative to their standard errors, which exceeds a 2:1 ratio. This significant variation may provide a statistical rationale for fitting more

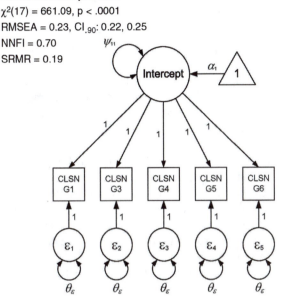

1: Random Intercept Model
$\chi^2(17) = 661.09$, p < .0001
RMSEA = 0.23, CI$_{.90}$: 0.22, 0.25
NNFI = 0.70
SRMR = 0.19

Figure 2.2   A Path Diagram Representing the Random Intercept Model.

NOTE: CLSN = Closeness with child.

complex models by, for example, including both time-varying and time-invariant covariates.

At the same time, the fit statistics show that the random intercept model does not provide an adequate fit to the data, as one might expect by examining Figure 2.1. The χ^2 test rejects the model at $p < .0001$, the RMSEA far exceeds the acceptable fit range (values less than .08 or so), and the model is characterized by large average residuals. Clearly, an intercept-only model is not appropriate for the mother–child closeness data. Next, a linear slope

TABLE 2.3
Model 1: Random Intercept Model

Parameter	Estimate
Mean intercept $\hat{\alpha}_1$	37.00 (0.09)
Intercept variance $\hat{\psi}_{11}$	5.27 (0.30)
Disturbance variance $\hat{\theta}_\varepsilon$	4.68 (0.11)

NOTE: Numbers in parentheses are standard errors of parameter estimates.

factor is introduced to account for the roughly linear trend observed in Figure 2.1.

Model 2: Fixed Intercept, Fixed Slope

In Model 2, we fix both the intercept and the slope, meaning that a single, average intercept parameter $(\hat{\alpha}_1)$ and linear slope parameter $(\hat{\alpha}_2)$ are estimated, ignoring any interindividual variation in the these aspects of change. The slope is included by adding a column to $\mathbf{\Lambda}_y$. This column now codes the slope factor and reflects two characteristics of the data. First, the loading corresponding to the first grade measure is coded 0 to place the origin of time at first grade. Second, the spacing between elements in the column reflects the fact that there was no measurement in the second grade. Thus, even though the elapsed time between the first and second measures is twice that between the second and third measures, the model still reflects linear growth because of the way in which time was coded (see Equation 2.5).

The latent growth curve specifications for Model 2 are presented in Figure 2.3. Matrix representations for the intercept and slope factors, their variances and covariances, and their means are as follows:

$$\mathbf{\Lambda}_y = \begin{bmatrix} 1 & 0 \\ 1 & 2 \\ 1 & 3 \\ 1 & 4 \\ 1 & 5 \end{bmatrix}, \tag{2.5}$$

$$\mathbf{\Psi} = \begin{bmatrix} 0 & \\ 0 & 0 \end{bmatrix}, \tag{2.6}$$

$$\mathbf{\alpha} = \begin{bmatrix} \alpha_1 \\ \alpha_2 \end{bmatrix}, \tag{2.7}$$

$$\mathbf{\Theta}_\varepsilon = \begin{bmatrix} \theta_\varepsilon & & & \\ 0 & \ddots & & \\ & & \ddots & \\ 0 & & 0 & \theta_\varepsilon \end{bmatrix}. \tag{2.8}$$

Because both the intercept and the slope are fixed, their variances and covariance are constrained to zero (hence $\mathbf{\Psi}$ contains zeroes). As in Model 1, the matrix $\mathbf{\Theta}_\varepsilon$ is constrained to represent the assumption of equal disturbance variances.

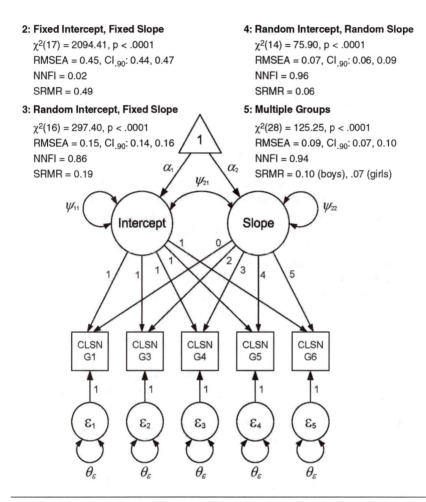

2: Fixed Intercept, Fixed Slope
$\chi^2(17) = 2094.41$, p < .0001
RMSEA = 0.45, CI$_{.90}$: 0.44, 0.47
NNFI = 0.02
SRMR = 0.49

3: Random Intercept, Fixed Slope
$\chi^2(16) = 297.40$, p < .0001
RMSEA = 0.15, CI$_{.90}$: 0.14, 0.16
NNFI = 0.86
SRMR = 0.19

4: Random Intercept, Random Slope
$\chi^2(14) = 75.90$, p < .0001
RMSEA = 0.07, CI$_{.90}$: 0.06, 0.09
NNFI = 0.96
SRMR = 0.06

5: Multiple Groups
$\chi^2(28) = 125.25$, p < .0001
RMSEA = 0.09, CI$_{.90}$: 0.07, 0.10
NNFI = 0.94
SRMR = 0.10 (boys), .07 (girls)

Figure 2.3   A Path Diagram Representing the General Linear Latent Growth Curve, With Random Intercept, Random Slope, Intercept–Slope Covariance, and Equal Disturbance Variances.

NOTE: CLSN = Closeness with child.

Results are reported in Table 2.4 and Figure 2.3. The new slope parameter estimate α_2 is significant and negative, reflecting the fact that closeness between mothers and children decreases over time during the elementary school years. However, the fit of Model 2 (see Figure 2.3) is much worse than that of Model 1. This poor fit comes from the way in which the intercept and slope factors are specified. Model 2 uses fixed intercept and slope factors. It constrains all mother–child pairs to share the same initial value of closeness and obliges all

TABLE 2.4
Model 2: Fixed Intercept, Fixed Slope

Parameter	Estimate
Mean intercept $\hat{\alpha}_1$	38.00 (0.09)
Mean slope $\hat{\alpha}_2$	−0.36 (0.03)
Disturbance variance $\hat{\theta}_\varepsilon$	9.57 (0.21)

NOTE: Numbers in parentheses are standard errors of parameter estimates.

pairs to decrease in closeness at precisely the same rate. People obviously differ, and this model does not take this into account. Another way to understand this lack of fit is to note that a fixed-intercept model implies that the between-person proportion of variance (the *intraclass correlation*, or ICC) is zero. To the extent that ICC deviates from zero in the data, the fixed-intercept model will fit more poorly. A random intercept model implies a nonzero ICC and so can account for some autocorrelation among the repeated measures. We address this issue first by relaxing the constraint on the intercept variance, or "freeing" the intercept (Model 3), and then by freeing both the intercept and slope (Model 4).

Model 3: Random Intercept, Fixed Slope

It is reasonable to suspect that not all mother–child pairs have the same level of closeness at Grade 1. However, the previous model with a fixed intercept was specified as if they did. Although we freed the intercept when we fit Model 1, we fixed it once grade was included in the form of slope factor loadings. A more realistic model would permit individuals to differ in intercept by permitting the intercept variance to be freely estimated. This slightly modified model represents interindividual variation in intercepts by estimating not only a mean intercept ($\hat{\alpha}_1$) but also an intercept variance ($\hat{\psi}_{11}$), indicating the degree to which individuals' intercepts vary about the population mean intercept. The parameter estimates from Model 3 (see Table 2.5) are similar to those from Model 2, with the average change in CLSN about −0.36 units per grade and an average intercept of approximately 38. The intercept variance ($\hat{\psi}_{11} = 5.37$) is significant, indicating that there is nontrivial variance between individuals in initial status. Allowing the intercept to be random across individuals—freeing only one parameter from Model 2—clearly improved model fit by a significant amount. As might be expected, this model fits much better than the previous fixed intercept model, with $\Delta\chi^2(1) = 1,797$.[5] However, there is still room for improvement, as indicated by the significant disturbance variance ($\hat{\theta}_\varepsilon = 4.21$). Just as it was reasonable to suppose that children vary at Grade 1 initial status, it is also reasonable to suppose that mother–child pairs vary in their rate of change over time.

TABLE 2.5
Model 3: Random Intercept, Fixed Slope

Parameter	Estimate
Mean intercept $\hat{\alpha}_1$	38.00 (0.10)
Mean slope $\hat{\alpha}_2$	−0.36 (0.02)
Intercept variance $\hat{\psi}_{11}$	5.37 (0.30)
Disturbance variance $\hat{\theta}_\varepsilon$	4.21 (0.10)

NOTE: Numbers in parentheses are standard errors of parameter estimates.

Note that the mean intercept and slope estimates in Model 3 are the same as those from Model 2; all we have done is permit the interindividual variability around the mean intercept. An interesting point is that the sum of the intercept variance and disturbance variance in Model 3 is equal to the disturbance variance from Model 2. In Model 2, the intercept variance was constrained to zero, forcing all the between-person variability to be expressed as disturbance variance. In the next model, both intercepts and slopes are permitted to vary.

Model 4: Random Intercept, Random Slope

Thus far, we have shown how to fit models with only fixed slopes. In general, however, there will be between-individual differences in both baseline level and in rate of change. Our previous models with fixed parameters each ignore some of this between-individual variability. To better reflect the nature of our data, we now specify both intercept and slope variance parameters to be random. In Model 4, every individual is allowed to have a different slope and a different intercept.[6] In addition to being more realistic in many contexts, this model allows estimation of the intercept–slope covariance (ψ_{21}). In our example, the intercept–slope covariance is interpreted as the degree to which mother–child closeness at Grade 1 is related to rate of change over time.

As in the previous models, the LGM representation of Model 4 is relatively simple. To specify this model, we free the variances of both intercept and slope factors and add an intercept–slope covariance parameter. Matrix Ψ therefore becomes

$$\Psi = \begin{bmatrix} \psi_{11} & \\ \psi_{21} & \psi_{22} \end{bmatrix}. \tag{2.9}$$

Estimating the parameters of Model 4 with LISREL yielded the estimates shown in Table 2.6. The intercept variance is large relative to the slope variance, and the intercept–slope covariance (0.25, corresponding to a correlation of 0.40) is significant. This indicates that children with higher intercepts have shallower negative slopes or that mother–child pairs who are closer at Grade 1 tend to decrease in closeness at a slower rate than those who are less close at Grade 1.

TABLE 2.6
Model 4: Random Intercept, Random Slope

Parameter	Estimate
Mean intercept $\hat{\alpha}_1$	38.00 (0.08)
Mean slope $\hat{\alpha}_2$	−0.36 (0.02)
Intercept variance $\hat{\psi}_{11}$	2.98 (0.29)
Slope variance $\hat{\psi}_{22}$	0.14 (0.02)
Intercept/slope covariance $\hat{\psi}_{21}$	0.25 (0.06)
Disturbance variance $\hat{\theta}_\varepsilon$	3.70 (0.10)

NOTE: Numbers in parentheses are standard errors of parameter estimates.

A chi-square difference test showed that this model with random intercept and random slope significantly improved fit over that of Model 3, which had only a random intercept, $\Delta\chi^2(2) = 221.5$, $p < .0001$. The RMSEA, NNFI, and SRMR fit indices indicate good fit as well. As noted, the significant positive covariance between intercept and slope implies that mother–child pairs who are closer in Grade 1 tend to experience less precipitous drops in closeness.

Returning to our comments about the interpretation of the intercept–slope covariance (ψ_{21}), before the reader concludes that children who have closer relationships with their mothers enjoy smaller decreases in closeness over the remaining elementary school years, we caution that the intercept–slope covariance might have been much less impressive had the zero point been defined at some other age. For example, if most children sampled had approximately identical mother–child closeness at kindergarten, then differences in slope alone would lead to the observed covariance when time is centered at Grade 1. Indeed, if the age variable is rescaled so that the intercept is defined at 2 years before Grade 1, a nonsignificant intercept/slope correlation of −.03 is obtained. This underscores the importance of the decision of where to place the origin of the time scale when fitting one's model.

Mehta and West (2000) note that if the linear LGM is an appropriate model for the data the true-score variance of the repeated measures will follow a quadratic pattern. Denoting time by t and the time origin by t^*,

$$\sigma^2_{\xi(t)} = \psi_{11} + \psi_{22}(t - t^*)^2 + 2\psi_{21}(t - t^*), \qquad (2.10)$$

where $\sigma^2_{\xi(t)}$ is the true score variance at time t and ψ_{11}, ψ_{22}, and ψ_{21} are, respectively, the population intercept variance, the slope variance, and the intercept–slope covariance. In other words, the collection of individual trajectories will resemble a bow tie or fan spread. In many situations, the point at which the between-person variability is minimized (the "knot" of the bow tie) is of interest. This point, which Hancock and Choi (2006) have termed the *aperture*, can be easily calculated as the choice of time origin that minimizes the intercept variance; that is,

$$a = a^* - \frac{\hat{\psi}_{21}}{\hat{\psi}_{22}}, \qquad (2.11)$$

where a^* is the occasion originally chosen for the time origin and $\hat{\psi}_{21}$ and $\hat{\psi}_{22}$ are, respectively, the estimated intercept–slope covariance and the slope variance.[7] The aperture is the point at which $\psi_{21} = 0$ (Mehta & West, 2000). Using the results of Model 4, the occasion at which children were most similar in mother–child closeness is $a = 0 - 0.2533/0.1366 = -1.85$, or nearly a year before kindergarten. Of course, caution in interpretation is warranted whenever the aperture falls outside the range of occasions for which data are observed, as it obliges the researcher to assume that a linear model is appropriate for those occasions. This may not be the case.

To summarize our progress so far, we have proceeded from estimating a null model through estimating a model with random intercept and slope. The random intercept model (Model 1) indicated that most variation occurred within individuals but that there also was a nonnegligible amount of variation between individuals. Model 2 showed what one might expect to find when between-individual variance is ignored and showed how constraining parameters to particular values can harm model fit when different individuals have different trajectories on the outcome measure. Model 3 built on Model 2 by freeing the intercept variance parameter. We found that allowing the intercept to vary across people resulted in a large improvement in model fit. The model with random intercepts and slopes (Model 4) performed much better than the previous, more constrained models (Models 2 and 3). In addition to improving overall fit, the advantages of Model 4 included discovering a significant positive covariance (ψ_{21}) between intercepts and slopes, implying that the rate at which closeness changes over time was related to closeness at Grade 1. We use Model 4 as the basis for all subsequent models. In Model 5, we examine the possibility that there are (child) gender differences in mother–child closeness trajectories.

Model 5: Multiple-Groups Analysis

The results from Model 4 imply that it is useful to think of individuals as having different intercepts and slopes. It is possible that some of this variance is systematically related to other variables of interest. For example, we can hypothesize and test group differences in mean intercept and slope for boys and girls (McArdle & Epstein, 1987). There are at least two ways to examine group differences in trajectories: (1) splitting the sample into two groups and estimating parameters in both groups simultaneously and (2) specifying the grouping variable as a predictor of both intercepts and slopes. Specifying a two-groups analysis in LISREL involves splitting the data file into two files based on gender and conducting a multisample analysis in which models are fit simultaneously to both data sets. The two models are specified in the same syntax file, and each model is as depicted in Figure 2.3. Equality constraints are imposed on key parameters in corresponding parameter matrices across groups to test hypotheses of group differences in those parameters. This multiple-groups method can be applied in principle to any number of groups, and models with different forms may be specified in the different groups. This method enables a novel approach to examining treatment effects and initial status × treatment interaction effects in longitudinal settings, as we discuss in the next chapter. Using group as a predictor variable is discussed in Model 6.

We follow the multiple-groups strategy for the closeness data, fitting separate models to boys and girls simultaneously with no cross-group constraints on model parameters. The results are reported in Table 2.7. NNFI was calculated using separately specified two-parameter null models for each group. Model fit is mediocre (RMSEA = .088; 90% confidence interval [CI] = {.072, .104}), permitting cautious interpretation of parameter estimates. All parameter estimates are significant for both boys and girls except for the intercept–slope covariance for girls ($\hat{\psi}_{21}$ = .14), which is notably lower than that for boys ($\hat{\psi}_{21}$ = .36). The correlations corresponding to these covariances are r = .22 (for girls) and r = .59 (for boys), indicating a much stronger relationship between initial status (at first grade) and change over time in mother–child closeness for boys than for girls.

Note that the intercept and the slope are lower for boys (37.85 and –0.38, respectively) than for girls (38.14 and –0.33, respectively), indicating that, on average, boys appear to start lower, and decrease at a faster pace, than girls. Given these apparent differences, if a researcher had substantive reason to test whether these differences were significant, one approach would be to constrain these parameters to equality across groups and look for a significant drop in model fit by means of a chi-square difference test. In this case, if an equality constraint is applied to intercept means (permitting slopes to vary), the result of the difference test is $\Delta\chi^2(1)$ = 3.11, p = .08,

TABLE 2.7

Model 5: Multiple Groups Analysis

Parameter	Estimate
Boys	
Mean intercept $\hat{\alpha}_1$	37.85 (0.12)
Mean slope $\hat{\alpha}_2$	−0.38 (0.03)
Intercept variance $\hat{\psi}_{11}$	3.03 (0.42)
Slope variance $\hat{\psi}_{22}$	0.12 (0.03)
Intercept/slope covariance $\hat{\psi}_{21}$	0.36 (0.08)
Disturbance variance $\hat{\theta}_\varepsilon$	3.78 (0.15)
Girls	
Mean intercept $\hat{\alpha}_1$	38.14 (0.11)
Mean slope $\hat{\alpha}_2$	−0.33 (0.03)
Intercept variance $\hat{\psi}_{11}$	2.90 (0.39)
Slope variance $\hat{\psi}_{22}$	0.15 (0.03)
Intercept/slope covariance $\hat{\psi}_{21}$	0.14 (0.08)
Disturbance variance $\hat{\theta}_\varepsilon$	3.63 (0.14)

NOTE: Numbers in parentheses are standard errors of parameter estimates.

indicating that the intercepts are not significantly different. If the equality constraint is instead applied to the slope means (permitting intercepts to vary), the difference test again is nonsignificant, $\Delta\chi^2(1) = 1.47$, $p = .23$, indicating that the slopes are not significantly different. Despite appearances, there is not enough evidence to suggest that boys and girls follow different linear trajectories in mother–child closeness from Grades 1 through 6. Other cross-group constraints are possible as well, of course—theory may suggest testing for differences in disturbance variances or intercept–slope covariances (ψ_{21}). A test of the hypothesis that ψ_{21} is equal for boys and girls also is inconclusive, $\Delta\chi^2(1) = 3.83$, $p > .05$.

For examples and further discussion of multiple-groups LGM, see Curran, Harford, and Muthén (1996), Curran, Muthén, and Harford (1998), McArdle (1989), and McArdle and Epstein (1987). We close this section by noting that we assume group membership is known (observable). If groups are assumed, but membership is uncertain, the researcher may be interested in growth mixture modeling, discussed in Chapter 3. Next, we illustrate an alternative method of investigating gender differences in closeness trajectories.

Model 6: The Conditional Growth Curve Model

Instead of running multiple-groups models, the analysis of gender differences in intercept and slope may be considerably simplified by including gender as an exogenous predictor (Level 2 predictor or *time-invariant covariate*) of both intercept and slope in a single-group analysis. Such predictors of random variables can be introduced to account for between-individual variance in the estimates of intercept and slope. The variance parameters were freed in Models 3 and 4. Because the intercept and slope variances can be considered unexplained individual differences, they potentially can be accounted for using this technique, which can equally well use categorical or continuous Level 2 predictors. This type of model is sometimes termed a *conditional LGM* (Tisak & Meredith, 1990; Willett & Sayer, 1994), whereas Models 1 to 5 could be termed *unconditional* (Singer & Willett, 2003). Although we chose only gender as a predictor, we could choose any number of variables, for example, variables designed to measure between-individual differences in ethnicity, socioeconomic status, or parental religiosity. A significant advantage of Model 6 over Model 5 is that, because it is unnecessary to divide the sample into groups, the time-invariant covariate may be either nominal (e.g., gender in this case) or continuous. A disadvantage is that the researcher must be able to assume invariance of some model parameters across groups. For example, whereas we were free to estimate different disturbance variances for boys and girls in Model 5, we are not free to do so in Model 6 without significant additional effort.

We demonstrate the use of a grouping variable (gender) as a predictor in Model 6. In this model, we include gender as a predictor of intercept with a fixed coefficient, β_1, which is interpreted as the mean effect of gender on intercept.[8] Gender is also included as a predictor of slope, with fixed coefficient β_2. When a time-invariant covariate is included as a predictor of slopes, the effect is often called a *cross-level interaction* because time (Level 1) interacts with the covariate (Level 2) to predict the repeated measures (Cronbach & Webb, 1975; Curran, Bauer, & Willoughby, 2004; Kreft & de Leeuw, 1998; Raudenbush & Bryk, 2002). Note that if the effect of age on mother–child closeness varies across individuals, and if gender partially explains interindividual variability in that effect, then the cross-level interaction has the same interpretation as a moderation effect in traditional multiple regression analysis.[9]

Figure 2.4 contains a path diagram including gender as a predictor of both intercept and slope. The variances of intercept and slope, as well as their covariance, were reconceptualized as residual variances and a residual covariance—that is, that portion of the variance and covariance not accounted for by gender. These residual parameters are depicted in Figure 2.4 as ψ_{11}, ψ_{22}, and ψ_{21}. The parameters β_1 and β_2 represent the effects of gender on intercept and slope, respectively. Results for this model are presented in Figure 2.4 and Table 2.8. NNFI was calculated using Model 0 as a null model, augmented by estimating the mean and variance of gender.

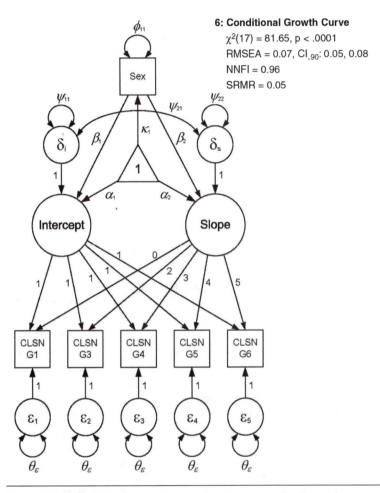

Figure 2.4　A Path Diagram Representing Gender as a Predictor of Individual Differences in Both Intercept and Slope.

NOTE: CLSN = Closeness with child.

Results for Model 6 show that the coefficient for predicting intercept from gender was −0.29; that is, mother–daughter pairs (coded 0) have higher average closeness scores than mother–son pairs (coded 1) at first grade, but not significantly higher. Mother–daughter pairs also showed less change over time than mother–son pairs, but not significantly less change. As we might expect, these results are consistent with those obtained in Model 5. For example, the difference between mean intercepts for girls and boys in Model 5 (see Table 2.7) was 37.85 − 38.14 = −0.29, equal to the

TABLE 2.8

Model 6: Conditional Growth Curve Model

Parameter	Estimate
Mean intercept $\hat{\alpha}_1$	38.14 (0.11)
Mean slope $\hat{\alpha}_2$	−0.33 (0.03)
Group effect on intercept $\hat{\beta}_1$	−0.29 (0.16)
Group effect on slope $\hat{\beta}_2$	−0.05 (0.04)
Intercept variance $\hat{\psi}_{11}$	2.96 (0.28)
Slope variance $\hat{\psi}_{22}$	0.14 (0.02)
Intercept/slope covariance $\hat{\psi}_{21}$	0.25 (0.06)

NOTE: Numbers in parentheses are standard errors of parameter estimates.

estimated fixed effect of gender, $\hat{\beta}_1$, in Model 6 (see Table 2.8). Similarly, the difference in slopes in Model 5 is −0.05, equal to the fixed effect of gender on slope, $\hat{\beta}_1$, obtained in Model 6. Because Models 5 and 6 are not completely identical (the disturbance variances are different across groups), results may not always resemble each other so closely. We note that this could easily be altered by imposing a cross-group equality constraint.

Treating time-invariant covariates as predictors of growth factors may lead to difficulties. The conditional growth curve model may be understood as a mediation model in which the growth factors are hypothesized to completely mediate the effect of the time-invariant covariate on the outcome variables, but complete mediation is rarely a tenable hypothesis. In Model 6, for example, by omitting paths linking child gender directly to closeness, the direct effects are implicitly constrained to zero. If these zero constraints are inappropriate, model fit will suffer and estimated parameters likely will be biased. An alternative strategy is to relax constraints on the direct effects (therefore estimating paths linking the covariate directly to each repeated measure) and instead constrain $\hat{\beta}_1$ and $\hat{\beta}_2$ to zero (Stoel, van den Wittenboer, & Hox, 2004). However, this model may not address a question of substantive interest. In addition, it should be borne in mind that interpretation of the effects of exogenous predictors on the intercept factor will vary with the scaling of time and the location of the time origin (Stoel, 2003; Stoel & van den Wittenboer, 2003).

Model 7: Parallel Process Model

It is possible to investigate the relationship between aspects of change specific to each of two repeated-measures variables, modeling growth processes in more than one variable. This procedure permits examination of relationships among aspects of change for different variables (McArdle, 1989). For example, a researcher may be interested in modeling growth in mother–child conflict and father–child conflict simultaneously to examine the relationship between the intercept of one and the slope of the other. This kind of model, referred to variously as a *parallel process model* (Cheong, MacKinnon, & Khoo, 2003), *multivariate change model* (MacCallum et al., 1997), *cross-domain individual growth model* (Sayer & Willett, 1998; Willett & Sayer, 1994, 1995), *multiple-domain model* (Byrne & Crombie, 2003), *fully multivariate latent trajectory model* (Curran & Hussong, 2003; Curran & Willoughby, 2003), *simultaneous growth model* (Curran et al., 1996); *bivariate growth model* (Aber & McArdle, 1991), or *associative LGM* (S. C. Duncan & Duncan, 1994; T. E. Duncan, Duncan, & Strycker, 2006; T. E. Duncan et al., 1999; Tisak & Meredith, 1990), follows easily from a simple random intercept, random slope model. A parallel process model contains two sets of intercepts and slopes, one set for each repeated-measures variable. The covariances among the intercepts and slopes are estimated as well (see Figure 2.5). For this example, we used mother–child closeness and mother–child conflict as the two dependent variables (see Table 2.9). The sample consisted of 849 children (433 girls and 416 boys) having complete data for both mother–child closeness and mother–child conflict. Model fit information can be found in Figure 2.5. NNFI was calculated by specifying as a null model a fixed intercept model for both closeness and conflict, permitting occasion-specific disturbances to covary.

Table 2.9 contains some interesting results, probably few of which will come as a surprise to parents of elementary-school-age children. First, parameter estimates related to mother–child closeness are, as expected, nearly identical to those from Model 4; any discrepancies can be attributed to the fact that the sample is slightly smaller for Model 7 due to missing data. Both closeness and conflict change over time, but in opposite directions, as indicated by their mean slope estimates. The estimates for the covariances among the intercepts and slopes are reported in the "Curve covariances" section of Table 2.9, and the correlations implied by these covariances are in the section "Curve correlations." The covariance of the intercepts ($\hat{\psi}_{31}$) is significantly negative, indicating that children who were particularly close to their mothers in first grade were also those who experienced the least conflict. Similarly, the slope covariance ($\hat{\psi}_{42}$) is significantly negative, indicating that children characterized by steeper decline in closeness tended to be those who experienced accelerated conflict as they aged. Finally, conflict intercepts were negatively associated with closeness

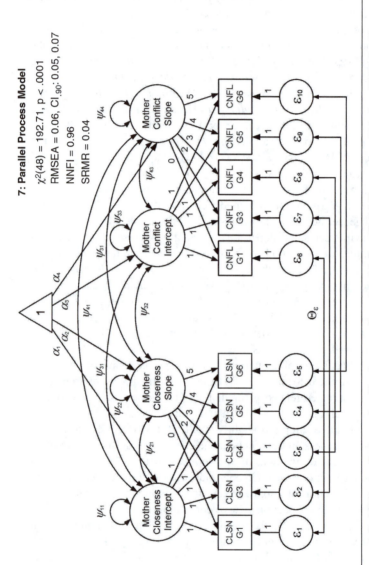

Figure 2.5   A Path Diagram Representing Simultaneous Growth in Mother–Child Closeness and Mother–Child Conflict.

NOTE: Intercepts and slopes from both variables are allowed to covary, as are disturbances for closeness and conflict measured at corresponding occasions. The disturbance variances for closeness were constrained to equality over time, as were the disturbance variances for conflict and the closeness–conflict disturbance covariances.

CLSN = Closeness with child; CNFL = Conflict with child

Within the figure:

7: Parallel Process Model

$\chi^2(48) = 192.71$, $p < .0001$
RMSEA = 0.06, CI$_{.90}$: 0.05, 0.07
NNFI = 0.96
SRMR = 0.04

TABLE 2.9
Model 7: Parallel Process Model

Parameter	Estimate
Mother–child closeness	
Mean intercept $\hat{\alpha}_1$	38.00 (0.08)
Mean slope $\hat{\alpha}_2$	−0.36 (0.02)
Intercept variance $\hat{\psi}_{11}$	2.99 (0.29)
Slope variance $\hat{\psi}_{22}$	0.14 (0.02)
Intercept/slope covariance $\hat{\psi}_{21}$	0.25 (0.06)
Mother–child conflict	
Mean intercept $\hat{\alpha}_3$	15.24 (0.20)
Mean slope $\hat{\alpha}_4$	0.30 (0.04)
Intercept variance $\hat{\psi}_{33}$	25.74 (1.61)
Slope variance $\hat{\psi}_{44}$	0.40 (0.06)
Intercept/slope covariance $\hat{\psi}_{43}$	−0.57 (0.23)
Curve covariances	
Intercept covariance $\hat{\psi}_{31}$	−3.88 (0.51)
CLSN intercept/CNFL slope covariance $\hat{\psi}_{41}$	0.13 (0.09)
CNFL intercept/CLSN slope covariance $\hat{\psi}_{32}$	−0.41 (0.12)
Slope covariance $\hat{\psi}_{42}$	−0.07 (0.02)
Curve correlations	
Intercept covariance	−0.44
CLSN intercept/CNFL slope covariance	0.12
CNFL intercept/CLSN slope covariance	−0.22
Slope covariance	−0.28

NOTE: Numbers in parentheses are standard errors of parameter estimates.
CLSN = Closeness with child; CNFL = Conflict with child.

slopes ($\hat{\psi}_{32}$), meaning that those first graders who demonstrated relatively more conflict with their mothers tended to experience more precipitous decreases in closeness as they got older.

Extensions to the basic parallel process model are possible. If the slopes associated with repeated measures of two variables are hypothesized to be not merely related but *causally* related, directional paths among growth factors may be specified. For example, Curran, Stice, and Chassin (1997) use a parallel process model in which both adolescent alcohol use and peer alcohol use change linearly over time. Age, gender, and parental alcoholism are used to predict aspects of change, and individual differences in intercepts from each repeated-measures variable (scaled to be at the initial measurement occasion) are used to predict variability in the other repeated-measures variable. Curran and Hussong (2002) model parallel growth in antisocial behavior and reading ability in children, predicting reading slopes with antisocial intercepts. Curran et al. (1996) specified a model in which the intercepts of alcohol use and bar patronage were hypothesized to affect one another's slopes. Raudenbush, Brennan, and Barnett (1995) used a similar approach to model predictors of simultaneous change in judgments of marital quality in husband/wife dyads, where each member of a dyad was measured at three yearly intervals. In addition, parallel processes in more than two repeated-measures variables may be specified.

Model 8: Cohort-Sequential Designs

Both the cross-sectional and longitudinal approaches potentially suffer from shortcomings when used to assess trajectories in single samples. Cross-sectional designs are sometimes prone to cohort or history effects that may mislead researchers into thinking a trend exists when one does not or masking a trend that actually exists. Longitudinal designs, on the other hand, are sometimes compromised by the threat of contamination due to repeated measurement of the same individuals. *Cohort-sequential designs* (Meredith & Tisak, 1990; Nesselroade & Baltes, 1979; Schaie, 1965, 1986; Tisak & Meredith, 1990), also called *accelerated longitudinal designs* (Miyazaki & Raudenbush, 2000; Raudenbush & Chan, 1992; Tonry, Ohlin, & Farrington, 1991) or the *method of convergence* (Bell, 1953, 1954; McArdle, 1988), have been suggested as a way to reduce the threat of these potential confounds by combining the longitudinal and cross-sectional approaches to examining developmental change. Cohort-sequential designs also greatly collapse the time needed to conduct longitudinal studies and reduce problems of attrition (Tonry et al., 1991). Consider the case in which age is the metric of time. Rather than follow the same sample of high school freshmen for 8 years through college, a researcher may instead elect to follow three cohorts (high school freshmen, high school juniors, and college freshmen) for only 4 years each. By employing multiple cohorts of subjects and measuring at only a few occasions within each cohort, a full trajectory for the entire time range of interest can be obtained. The cohort-sequential design is more appropriately thought of as an efficient data collection strategy than as a model, although this strategy leads to some interesting modeling options.

To demonstrate analysis of cohort-sequential data in our example, we created two artificial cohorts. We first randomly separated our data into two groups and then deleted data to mimic the pattern of data that might be gathered in a true cohort-sequential design. For Cohort 1, we deleted all measurements for children in Grade 6, and for Cohort 2, we deleted all measurements for children in Grade 1. This resulted in a data set in which children in Cohort 1 provided data for Grades 1, 3, 4, and 5, and children in Cohort 2 provided data for Grades 3 through 6. In randomly assigning cases to each cohort and deleting a portion of the data, our sample size was reduced to 893 ($n_1 = 426$, $n_2 = 467$). In practice, of course, data from these two cohorts would be collected concurrently over a single span of 5 years. Even less overlap is probably acceptable.

Cohort-sequential data can be examined in either of two ways. First, the researcher can aggregate the data and perform a single-group analysis. This approach involves treating uncollected data for each cohort as MCAR, which ordinarily is a safe assumption because such data are missing by design (T. E. Duncan et al., 1999; B. Muthén, 2000). Alternatively, the researcher can consider the cohorts as separate groups and perform a multiple-groups analysis (McArdle & Hamagami, 1992). This approach is similar to Model 5, with data separated by cohort and all corresponding parameters constrained to equality across cohorts. The multiple-groups option derives from one approach to dealing with missing data in which a relatively small number of "missingness" patterns are identifiable (Allison, 1987; T. E. Duncan et al., 1999; McArdle & Bell, 2000; McArdle & Hamagami, 1991; B. Muthén et al., 1987). B. Muthén (2000) described the implementation of cohort-sequential designs using these two approaches. It should be noted that treating cohorts as separate groups may lead to estimation problems in some circumstances (T. E. Duncan et al., 1999). With small groups, there may even be more measurement occasions than subjects, resulting in the necessary removal of some data, leaving some measurement occasions unrepresented. Here, our sample is quite large, so this issue is not a concern. We demonstrate both the single-group and multiple-groups approaches.

The specifications for the single-group approach are the same as for Model 4, and the path diagram is therefore that in Figure 2.3. The only difference here is that all subjects in Cohort 1 have missing values for Grade 6, and those in Cohort 2 have missing values for Grade 1. The results (see Table 2.10) are similar to those obtained for Model 4, although, as one would expect given the smaller sample size and the missing data, the standard errors are slightly larger. In spite of this, however, the results support the same conclusions drawn from analysis of the larger sample. The estimated mean closeness score at first grade is $\hat{\alpha}_1 = 37.99$, and the mean slope is $\hat{\alpha}_2 = -0.35$. Both are similar to the Model 4 estimates, as were the variances and covariance of the intercept and the slope.

The multiple-groups cohort-sequential approach is similar to the two-group analysis demonstrated earlier (Model 5), with all parameters constrained to equality across cohorts, including intercept and slope means. It is important to exercise care in specifying the equality constraints. In our analysis, each data file contains only those variables for which participants provide data. Therefore, the data file for Cohort 1 has only four variables,

TABLE 2.10

Model 8: Cohort-Sequential Design

Parameter	Single-Group Estimate	Multiple-Group Estimate
Mean intercept $\hat{\alpha}_1$	37.99 (0.10)	37.95 (0.13)
Mean slope $\hat{\alpha}_2$	−0.35 (0.03)	−0.36 (0.04)
Intercept variance $\hat{\psi}_{11}$	3.73 (0.43)	3.73 (0.43)
Slope variance $\hat{\psi}_{22}$	0.10 (0.03)	0.10 (0.03)
Intercept/slope covariance $\hat{\psi}_{21}$	0.21 (0.10)	0.21 (0.10)
Disturbance variance $\hat{\theta}_\varepsilon$	3.77 (0.12)	3.78 (0.12)

NOTE: Numbers in parentheses are standard errors of parameter estimates.

corresponding to measurements at Grades 1, 3, 4, and 5. Similarly, the data file for Cohort 2 contains measurements for only Grades 3 through 6. The variable for closeness at Grade 4 in Cohort 1 is the third repeated measure, whereas for Cohort 2 it is the second. The factor loading matrices for the two cohorts, then, are

$$\mathbf{\Lambda}_1 = \begin{bmatrix} 1 & 0 \\ 1 & 2 \\ 1 & 3 \\ 1 & 4 \end{bmatrix}, \tag{2.12}$$

$$\mathbf{\Lambda}_2 = \begin{bmatrix} 1 & 2 \\ 1 & 3 \\ 1 & 4 \\ 1 & 5 \end{bmatrix}. \tag{2.13}$$

The corresponding path diagram is shown in Figure 2.6.

The resulting parameter estimates on the right-hand side of Table 2.10 are highly similar to those obtained from the single-group analysis. For additional examples of the multiple-groups cohort-sequential approach, see reports by Aber and McArdle (1991), Anderson (1993), Baer and Schmitz (2000), Buist, Deković, Meeus, and van Aken (2002), T. E. Duncan, Duncan, and Hops (1993), S. C. Duncan, Duncan, and Hops (1996), and McArdle and Anderson (1990).

Note that NNFI is not provided for the single-group cohort-sequential design because some data are treated as missing. To permit the use of ML estimation with access to all ML-based fit indices, we recommend using the multiple-groups approach if complete data are available within each group, using covariances and means as input data for each cohort. If some cases

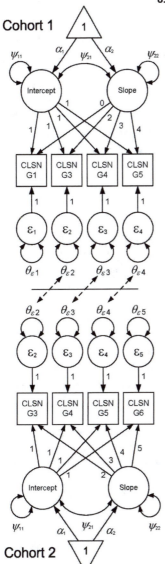

8: Cohort-Sequential Design

Single group

$\chi^2(14) = 73.16$, p < .0001

RMSEA = 0.07, CI$_{.90}$: 0.05, 0.08

Multiple group

$\chi^2(20) = 78.95$, p < .0001

RMSEA = 0.08, CI$_{.90}$: 0.06, 0.10

NNFI = 0.96

SRMR = 0.07 (Cohort 1)

          0.09 (Cohort 2)

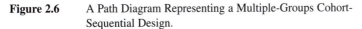

Figure 2.6   A Path Diagram Representing a Multiple-Groups Cohort-Sequential Design.

NOTE: The horizontal line represents the division between the two simultaneously estimated models. Parameters with identical labels and subscripts are constrained to equality across models.

CLSN = Closeness with child.

have missing data, we recommend using FIML to take advantage of missing data techniques that use all available data. It is rarely appropriate to discard data. In addition, if it is desired to estimate disturbance variances separately within each cohort, the multiple-groups approach is preferable.

The multiple-groups approach to testing cohort-sequential designs can be used explicitly to test for cohort effects, such as cohort differences in mean intercept or slope, by means of $\Delta\chi^2$ tests (Anderson, 1993; Meredith & Tisak, 1990). The single-group approach also may be used to test for cohort effects by including cohort as a dummy-variable predictor of intercept and slope (Raudenbush & Chan, 1992) and noting significant effects, but this model imposes the assumption of equal disturbance variances across cohorts.[10]

Model 9: Time-Varying Covariates

Earlier we defined TVCs as variables measured repeatedly and used to predict repeated measures of an outcome variable. Very little attention has been devoted to the treatment of TVCs in the LGM context, although much has been written on the subject of TVCs in the context of multilevel modeling. There are two ways to conceive of TVCs in LGM. These two methods address subtly different questions. The first, suggested by B. Muthén (1993) and illustrated or used in articles by George (2003), Bijleveld and van der Kamp (1998), and Curran and colleagues (Curran & Hussong, 2002, 2003; Curran & Willoughby, 2003; Curran et al., 1998; B. O. Muthén & Curran, 1997), is to include TVCs directly in the model as repeated exogenous predictors of the outcome, as in Figure 2.7. The β parameters in this model are interpreted as occasion-specific effects of the covariate, or as the ability of the covariate to predict occasion-specific deviations in the outcome. In this approach, the effect of a TVC may vary across time, but not across individuals. Alternatively, the β parameters could be constrained to equality to represent the hypothesis that the covariate effect remains stable over occasions. Either way, this model reflects growth in the repeated-measure variable controlling for occasion-specific effects of the TVC.

We fit the model in Figure 2.7 to the closeness data, treating mother–child conflict as a TVC measured concurrently with closeness. The results are reported in Table 2.11 and in Figure 2.7. NNFI was computed by augmenting the null model in Model 0 by estimating the means and variances of the five repeated measures of the TVC. The time-specific effect of conflict on closeness remained between -0.15 and -0.13 for all examined grades, indicating that, at each occasion, conflict tended to be negatively related to closeness after partialing out individual differences accounted for by the intercept and slope factors. To claim that this relationship is *causal* would be unjustified without first satisfying the criteria for establishing a causal relationship.

An alternative method of including TVCs in growth curve models makes use of definition variables. This approach differs somewhat from standard practice in SEM, but is equivalent to standard methods of including TVCs in multilevel modeling (e.g., Raudenbush & Chan, 1993). The variable *time* (or *age*, etc.) itself can be considered a TVC because time varies across repeated measures of the outcome. If definition variables can accommodate

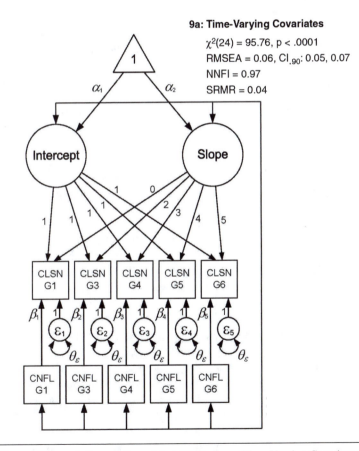

9a: Time-Varying Covariates

$\chi^2(24) = 95.76$, p < .0001
RMSEA = 0.06, CI$_{.90}$: 0.05, 0.07
NNFI = 0.97
SRMR = 0.04

Figure 2.7   A Growth Curve Model Including a Time-Varying Covariate of the Sort Suggested by B. Muthén (1993).

NOTE: Although not individually depicted, all variances and covariances among the intercept factor, slope factor, and TVC variables are estimated.

CLSN = Closeness with child; CNFL = Conflict with child.

48

TABLE 2.11
Model 9a: Time-Varying Covariates

Parameter	Estimate
Mean intercept $\hat{\alpha}_1$	40.17 (0.41)
Mean slope $\hat{\alpha}_2$	−0.36 (0.12)
Intercept variance $\hat{\psi}_{11}$	2.41 (0.25)
Slope variance $\hat{\psi}_{22}$	0.13 (0.02)
Intercept/slope covariance $\hat{\psi}_{21}$	0.20 (0.05)
Disturbance variance $\hat{\theta}_\varepsilon$	3.52 (0.10)
Conflict effect (G1) $\hat{\beta}_1$	−0.15 (0.03)
Conflict effect (G3) $\hat{\beta}_2$	−0.13 (0.01)
Conflict effect (G4) $\hat{\beta}_3$	−0.13 (0.01)
Conflict effect (G5) $\hat{\beta}_4$	−0.13 (0.01)
Conflict effect (G6) $\hat{\beta}_5$	−0.13 (0.02)

NOTE: Numbers in parentheses are standard errors of parameter estimates.

different occasions of measurement across individuals, they can also be used to model the effects of any other TVC in a similar manner. An additional slope factor is added to the model to represent the TVC. Values of the TVC are inserted into individual data vectors, essentially giving each individual or Level 2 unit a unique Λ_y matrix. In this approach, the effect of a TVC can vary across individuals, but not across time. That is, a mean effect of the TVC across individuals is estimated and, if desired, the variance of the TVC's slope factor (and covariances with other aspects of change) also can be estimated. This approach requires raw data as input.

For example, consider the model in Figure 2.8. At each occasion of measurement (grade), each individual also provided data on mother–child conflict (the TVC). Three individual data vectors are illustrated. Numbers in diamonds represent contents of each individual data vector for the TVC. Similar notation can be found in Mehta and West (2000, p. 34). Using this method, multiple TVCs may be included by using a different slope factor for each covariate. Interactions among TVCs (e.g., the interaction between grade and mother–child conflict) may be investigated by including slope factors containing loadings equal to the products of slope loadings for the involved covariates. For example, in Figure 2.8, the loadings on the interaction factor for Person 1 would be 0, 20, 21, 72, and 80. Cross-level interactions between time-invariant and time-varying covariates may be specified by including predictors of TVC slope factors. Models specified this way are equivalent to multilevel models with Level 1 predictors.

Fitting the model in Figure 2.8 to our closeness and conflict data yielded the results reported in Table 2.12. Because raw data were used as input, fit indices such as RMSEA and NNFI are not provided. Because Mx was used

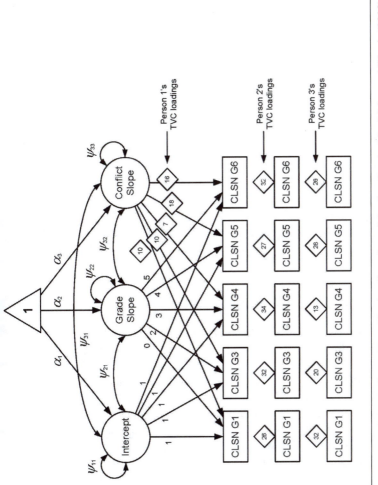

Figure 2.8   A Growth Curve Model Including a Time-Varying Covariate of the Sort Inspired by Mehta and West's (2000) Treatment of Time.

NOTE: A growth model may also be applied to the repeated measures of the covariate. Disturbance variances are present but not illustrated.

CLSN = Closeness with child; TVC = Time-varying covariate.

for this analysis, we are able to provide likelihood-based 95% confidence intervals[11] for each parameter estimate rather than the usual standard errors (Mx does not provide standard errors as a default option and, in fact, warns against their use with parameters having nonnormal sampling distributions, such as variances). All parameter estimates, save two, are statistically significant.

TABLE 2.12
Model 9b: Time-Varying Covariates

Parameter	Estimate	95% Confidence Interval
Mean intercept $\hat{\alpha}_1$	40.12	{39.82, 40.43}
Mean grade slope $\hat{\alpha}_2$	−0.31	{−0.35, −0.27}
Mean conflict slope $\hat{\alpha}_3$	−0.14	{−0.16, −0.12}
Intercept variance $\hat{\psi}_{11}$	4.93	{3.40, 6.72}
Grade slope variance $\hat{\psi}_{22}$	0.11	{0.08, 0.15}
Conflict slope variance $\hat{\psi}_{33}$	0.02	{0.02, 0.03}
Intercept/grade slope covariance $\hat{\psi}_{21}$	0.11	{−0.08, 0.29}
Intercept/conflict slope covariance $\hat{\psi}_{31}$	−0.28	{−0.39, −0.19}
Grade/conflict slope covariance $\hat{\psi}_{32}$	0.00	{−0.01, 0.01}
Disturbance variance $\hat{\theta}_\varepsilon$	3.28	{3.09, 3.48}

Model 10: Polynomial Growth Curves

The trajectories we have examined with growth curve models have been simple linear functions of *time* or *age*. The LGM user is not limited to linear functions, however. The framework presented thus far can accommodate any trajectories that are *linear in parameters* and *nonlinear in variables*. That is, basic LGM models can accommodate any trajectory in which the parameters of growth act as simple linear weights associated with transformations of the time metric. A common example is the quadratic latent growth curve (MacCallum et al., 1997; Meredith & Tisak, 1990; Stoolmiller, 1995) illustrated in Figure 2.9. In Figure 2.9, the loadings associated with the quadratic slope factor are the squares of the loadings associated with the linear slope factor. The mean of the quadratic slope (α_3) represents the degree of quadratic curvature in the trajectory.

We fit the quadratic growth curve in Figure 2.9 to the closeness data. Results are reported in Table 2.13 and Figure 2.9. The mean of the quadratic component is not significant ($\hat{\alpha}_3 = -0.019$, $p = .077$). A χ^2 difference test reveals that, compared with a purely linear model, the improvement in model fit is negligible ($\Delta\chi^2(1) = 3.12$, $p = .078$). Had there been a theoretical motive to do so, we might also have chosen to permit the quadratic

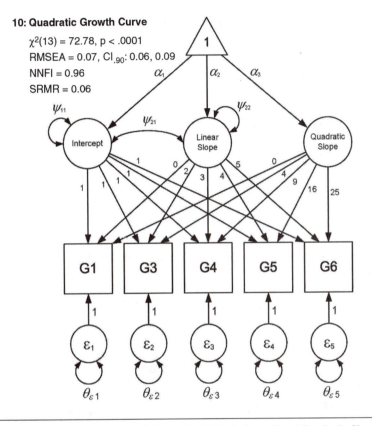

Figure 2.9   A Latent Growth Curve Model Including a Fixed Quadratic Slope Factor.

slope factor to vary randomly and to covary with the intercept and linear slope factors (Willett & Sayer, 1994) despite the lack of a mean quadratic effect. In fact, doing so results in a significant improvement in fit, but it is likely that the added complexity, in the form of three additional free parameters, overfits the data by absorbing random variability.

All too frequently, we suspect, quadratic growth curves are fit when a linear LGM does not fit adequately. We caution against this use of a quadratic model as capitalizing on possibly idiosyncratic characteristics of the particular sample under scrutiny. We suspect that there are few theories in the social sciences that naturally lead to predictions of nonlinear change that specifically imply a quadratic trend. Assuming there are enough repeated measures so that additional variance and covariance parameters will be

TABLE 2.13
Model 10: Polynomial Growth Curve

Parameter	Estimate
Mean intercept $\hat{\alpha}_1$	37.94 (0.09)
Mean linear slope $\hat{\alpha}_2$	−0.26 (0.06)
Mean quadratic slope $\hat{\alpha}_3$	−0.02 (0.01)
Intercept variance $\hat{\psi}_{11}$	2.98 (0.29)
Linear slope variance $\hat{\psi}_{22}$	0.14 (0.02)
Intercept/linear covariance $\hat{\psi}_{21}$	0.25 (0.06)
Disturbance variance $\hat{\theta}_\varepsilon$	3.70 (0.10)

NOTE: Numbers in parentheses are standard errors of parameter estimates.

identified, any number of polynomial growth factors may be added. However, a proper theoretical rationale must exist for adding these aspects of change.

It is possible to specify functional forms other than polynomial curves. Later we discuss structured latent curves, extensions to traditional growth curve models that can accommodate more complex functional forms that are *nonlinear in parameters*, in which the parameters of growth are no longer necessarily simple linear weights. One example is the exponential function commonly used to model population growth.

Model 11: Unspecified Trajectories

In the models described to this point, the function relating the outcome variable to time was completely defined. For example, in Figure 2.3, the paths from the slope factor to the measured variables are fixed in a linear progression, from 0 through 5, corresponding to a linear influence of grade on mother–child closeness. A creative extension of LGM involves the creation of *shape factors*, aspects of change for which the shape of the growth function (and therefore the factor loadings) are unknown and must be estimated from the data rather than specified a priori by the researcher (Meredith & Tisak, 1990). For example, we could replace the linear factor with a shape factor in Model 4, constrain the first and last loadings for this new factor to 0 and 1,[12] respectively, and estimate the remaining three loadings (λ_{22}, λ_{32}, and λ_{42}) using 0 and 1 as anchors. The estimated loadings would reveal the shape of the longitudinal trend. Although the free loadings are not proportions per se, even roughly linear growth should result in loadings that monotonically increase from 0 to 1. Alternatively, the first two loadings can be constrained to 0 and 1, in which case subsequent intervals can be interpreted by using the change occurring between the first two occasions as a benchmark (Hancock & Lawrence, 2006; Stoel, 2003). Models with shape factors are sometimes called *completely latent* (Curran & Hussong, 2002, 2003; McArdle, 1989), *fully latent* (Aber & McArdle, 1991), or *unspecified* (T. E. Duncan et al., 2006; Lawrence & Hancock, 1998; Stoolmiller, 1995; J. Wang, 2004) because the trajectory has not been specified a priori. This model is more exploratory than previously discussed models in that the researcher is not testing hypotheses about specific trajectories. Rather, the data are used to gain insight into what kind of trajectory might be appropriate. Freeing some of the loadings on a linear slope factor to create a shape factor allows direct comparison of the two models using a nested-model χ^2 difference test, essentially a test of departure from linearity. Good examples of unspecified trajectory models are provided by T. E. Duncan et al. (1993), T. E. Duncan, Tildesley, Duncan, and Hops (1995), and McArdle and Anderson (1990).

We applied an unspecified trajectory model to our mother–child closeness data, anchoring the first and fifth loadings to 0 and 5, respectively, to mirror our previous scaling of time (see Figure 2.10). A χ^2 difference test comparing Model 11 with Model 4 resulted in a nonsignificant difference ($\Delta\chi^2(3) = 2.68, p = .44$), indicating that a linear trend is sufficient to model the mother–child closeness data. This conclusion is bolstered by the fact that the loadings followed a nearly perfectly linear trend even without being constrained, as illustrated in Figure 2.11.

Summary

In this chapter, we described several latent growth curve models. Beginning with a basic null model, each model was applied in turn to the same data set to illustrate use of the models in practice. Beyond the basic linear LGM with random intercepts and random slopes, we showed how the model could be extended to handle multiple groups, predictors of intercept and slope factors, and growth in more than one outcome variable or more than one age cohort. We showed how TVCs may be added to a growth curve model and how polynomial or unspecified nonlinear trajectories can be modeled.

We want to emphasize that the researcher need not be restricted to investigating the progression of models presented in this chapter. If theory or past research suggests that a random intercepts, random slopes model is appropriate, then there is little reason to fit a simpler model. Likewise, if there is reason to expect a Level 2 predictor to explain individual differences in the quadratic component of a polynomial trend, it is straightforward and

54

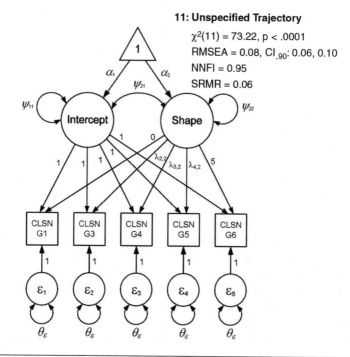

11: Unspecified Trajectory

$\chi^2(11) = 73.22$, p < .0001
RMSEA = 0.08, CI$_{.90}$: 0.06, 0.10
NNFI = 0.95
SRMR = 0.06

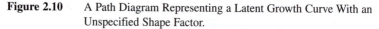

Figure 2.10   A Path Diagram Representing a Latent Growth Curve With an
Unspecified Shape Factor.

NOTE: CLSN = Closeness with child.

appropriate to combine Models 6 and 10 rather than beginning with one model or the other. In short, it is important to always look to theory first. If theory is not sufficiently specific to suggest models to be investigated, then the exploratory strategy illustrated in this chapter—beginning with a null model, subsequently including a linear slope factor, and adding random effects and predictors—can be useful in helping the researcher to understand the data and appropriately model change over time.

Notes

1. We use complete data in this book for pedagogical simplicity and because the full array of SEM fit indices is available when complete data are used. The data used in subsequent analyses are provided along with syntax at http://www.quantpsy.org/.
2. LISREL is available from Scientific Software International (http://www.ssicentral.com/); Mx is available from Virginia Commonwealth University (http://www.vcu.edu/mx/); and Mplus is available from L. K. Muthén & Muthén (http://www.statmodel.com/).

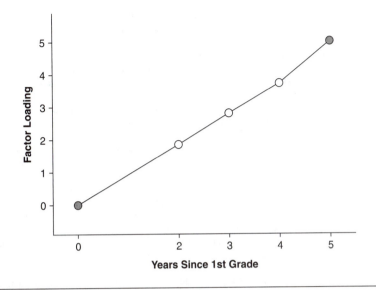

Figure 2.11   A Plot of Factor Loadings Versus Years Since the First Grade.

NOTE: Open circles represent estimated loadings. Closed circles represent fixed loadings used to anchor the estimation of the remaining loadings. Although the factor loadings follow a positive linear trend, they actually describe a *downward* trajectory because the slope mean is negative.

3. Throughout this book, we constrain the disturbance variances to equality for pedagogical simplicity and because it is reasonable to suppose that residual variability in mother–child closeness remains stable over time. This equality constraint is not required, assuming there are enough repeated measures to identify these parameters. Indeed, a strength of the LGM approach is that we can explicitly model heteroskedasticity—or any of a number of other disturbance covariance structures—by estimating different residual variances across occasions (Willett & Sayer, 1994). All things being equal, however, we recommend that preference be given to modeling homoscedasticity (equal disturbance variances) whenever possible to maximize parsimony, and because permitting residual variances to differ by occasion can sometimes mask or "soak up" nonlinearity in the trajectory, yielding deceptively good fit.

4. Syntax for this model, and for most subsequent models, is provided at our Web site (http://www.quantpsy.org/).

5. This is the nested model test we mentioned earlier, in which the difference in χ^2 values for the two models is itself treated as a χ^2 statistic with degrees of freedom equal to the difference in *df* for the two nested models.

6. To be clear, separate intercepts and slopes are not actually estimated in this procedure; rather, the model imposes a multivariate normal distribution on the latent variables and yields estimates of the means, variances, and covariances of those distributions.

7. Alternatively (and equivalently), the aperture can be directly estimated as a model parameter in some SEM programs by constraining ψ_{21} to zero and constraining the slope factors to their original fixed values minus an aperture parameter.

8. In this model, and later in Model 9, we make use of β parameters, which are elements of a matrix of path coefficients (**B**) from the full structural equation model not discussed in Chapter 1 (Bollen, 1989).

9. Because of this similarity, cross-level interactions in multilevel modeling may be decomposed, probed, and plotted according to guidelines stated by Aiken and West (1991). See Curran, Bauer, and Willoughby (2004) and Preacher, Curran, and Bauer (2006) for discussion.

10. These two approaches to testing for cohort effects are directly analogous to the two approaches for examining the effects of exogenous predictors of change discussed in Models 5 and 6.

11. Likelihood-based CIs are computed by determining the values a parameter must adopt for model fit to worsen by a given amount. For example, 95% CIs are formed by moving the parameter value away from the ML estimate in small steps—reoptimizing the model each time—until the ML fit function increases by 3.84 χ^2 units (3.84 is the critical value of χ^2 when $df = 1$) (Neale et al., 2003; Neale & Miller, 1997). This method of creating CIs can be time-consuming due to the amount of CPU-intensive reoptimization required, but likelihood-based CIs have several advantages over standard errors, which assume normality (typically untrue of variance parameters, for example), require t tests that are not invariant to reparameterization, and sometimes yield nonsensical results for bounded parameters. Standard errors are still de rigueur when reporting parameter estimates, but we predict that likelihood-based CIs will become more popular because of their desirable characteristics, particularly as computers improve in cost and computational efficiency.

12. Two loadings must be constrained for this model to be identified. Any two loadings will suffice, as long as they are constrained to different values.

CHAPTER 3. SPECIALIZED EXTENSIONS

We have by no means exhausted the possibilities of LGM with the examples presented thus far. As scientific hypotheses become more complex, the models used to represent those hypotheses will show a concomitant increase in complexity and flexibility. In this chapter, we present several interesting and useful extensions and specialized applications of traditional growth curve models that take advantage of both recent advancements in statistical theory and recent software improvements. These applications include growth mixture models, piecewise growth curve models, modeling change in latent variables, structured latent curve models, autoregressive latent trajectory models, and modeling change in categorical outcomes.

Growth Mixture Models

In most of the models described to this point, we assumed that a single latent trajectory would be sufficient to characterize the pattern of change in the population while allowing for random error in that trajectory. In Model 5, we noted that discrete classes (such as male and female) could follow different latent trajectories. That is, separate growth trajectories may be estimated simultaneously within each of several known groups, with or without cross-group constraints on key parameters. However, it need not be the case that the classification variable is observed; it is quite possible that latent (unobserved) classes could give rise to heterogeneous trajectories. If more than one such class exists, but only one trajectory is specified, significant bias likely will be introduced and the resulting trajectory may misrepresent all trajectory classes (Sterba, Prinstein, & Cox, 2007; von Eye & Bergman, 2003).

If it is reasonable to assume the existence of latent sources of heterogeneity in trajectories, then the researcher may wish to employ *latent growth mixture modeling* (LGMM). In a growth curve mixture model, the population is assumed to consist of a mixture of K homogeneous subgroups, each with its own distinct developmental trajectory. There are two popular approaches to fitting growth curve mixture models (B. Muthén, 2001; Nagin, 1999; Nagin & Tremblay, 2001). Both versions involve regressing the latent intercept and slope factors onto a latent classification variable, and both versions permit the form of the trajectory to differ across classes (i.e., the trajectory could be linear in one class and quadratic in another). The primary difference between the two approaches is that Muthén's

(2001) permits variability in trajectories within classes, whereas Nagin's (1999) requires trajectory variability to lie at the between-class level. As a consequence, Nagin's (1999) method usually results in concluding that more latent classes exist than does Muthén's (2001).

One potential disadvantage of LGMM is that growth mixture models may lead researchers to believe that multiple homogeneous subgroups exist, when in fact only one group exists in which the data are distributed nonnormally or follow a nonlinear trend (Bauer & Curran, 2003a). In other words, the groups identified as a result of growth mixture modeling may not represent true groups, but rather components of a mixture distribution of trajectories that together approximate a single nonnormal distribution. Because the existence of heterogeneous subpopulations is a basic assumption of LGMM, the method cannot *prove* that there are *K* classes, just as the implicit extraction of one class in traditional LGM does not *prove* there is only one population trajectory (Bauer & Curran, 2003a, 2003b, 2004). More generally, there is considerable evidence that a variety of assumption violations will produce artifactual latent classes (Bauer, 2005, 2007).

Growth mixture models are not easy to understand or to implement. Improper solutions are common, overextraction of classes is routine, and parameter estimation tends to be sensitive to starting values. In addition, model evaluation and model selection are not straightforward. Models specifying different numbers of classes may be compared using information criteria such as the Bayesian information criterion (BIC), but the application of information criteria to mixture models remains an active area of research. Several subjective decisions need to be made at various points in the process, and mixture modeling typically requires much larger sample sizes than standard applications. In addition, although assumption violations are always a potential hazard in latent variable analysis, LGMM is particularly vulnerable. Violation of distributional assumptions and misspecification of trajectory form can result in the extraction of multiple classes even in a homogeneous population. Nevertheless, there are exciting possibilities afforded by these methods. For example, LGMM can be used to test developmental theories involving equifinality, in which different initial conditions result in the same outcome, and multifinality, in which identical initial conditions lead to different outcomes (e.g., Cicchetti & Rogosch, 1996).

LGMM is an area of active study, and advances continue to be made. For example, Klein and Muthén (2006) describe an extension to LGMM that permits heterogeneity in growth to depend on initial status and time-invariant covariates. Their method results in more accurate prediction intervals than standard LGM without being as highly parameterized as LGMM. The method is not yet implemented in widely available software.

At present, growth mixture modeling can be accomplished with MECOSA for GAUSS (Arminger, Wittenberg, & Schepers, 1996), Mplus (L. K. Muthén & Muthén, 1998–2006), Mx (Neale et al., 2003), and SAS PROC TRAJ (Jones, Nagin, & Roeder, 2001). Mplus is currently the most flexible of these applications. Interested researchers are referred to Bauer (2005, 2007), Bauer and Curran (2003a, 2003b, 2004), T. E. Duncan et al. (2006), Li, Duncan, Duncan, and Acock (2001), and M. Wang and Bodner (2007).

Piecewise Growth

Suppose theory or prior research suggests that growth should proceed at a different—but still linear—rate during the middle school years than during the elementary school years (due to differences in school funding, for example). Both phases of growth may be modeled within a single LGM using a *piecewise growth model* (T. E. Duncan et al., 2006; Sayer & Willett, 1998) or *discontinuity design* (Hancock & Lawrence, 2006). Piecewise growth models are specified by including two or more linear slope factors in one model. For example, if we had continued to collect data for Grades 7, 8, and 9 and hypothesized that growth would decelerate in the middle school years, the loading matrix Λ_y may look like Equation 3.1:

$$\Lambda_y = \begin{bmatrix} 1 & 0 & 0 \\ 1 & 2 & 0 \\ 1 & 3 & 0 \\ 1 & 4 & 0 \\ 1 & 5 & 0 \\ 1 & 5 & 1 \\ 1 & 5 & 2 \\ 1 & 5 & 3 \end{bmatrix}. \tag{3.1}$$

In Equation 3.1, the first column represents the intercept, the second column represents linear growth up to the sixth grade (the fifth occasion of measurement), and the mean of the first linear slope factor will represent the rate of linear growth characterizing the elementary school years. The third column of Λ_y represents linear growth during the middle school years, treating the last year of elementary school as a second origin for the time scale. The mean of the second linear slope factor will reflect the middle school rate of growth. An alternative (but statistically equivalent) specification might be to use the Λ_y matrix in Equation 3.2 (Hancock & Lawrence, 2006). In Equation 3.2, the first slope factor represents linear growth across Grades 1 to 9, and the second slope factor represents any *additional* linear change, beginning in Grade 7, above and beyond that captured by the second linear slope:

$$\Lambda_y = \begin{bmatrix} 1 & 0 & 0 \\ 1 & 2 & 0 \\ 1 & 3 & 0 \\ 1 & 4 & 0 \\ 1 & 5 & 0 \\ 1 & 6 & 1 \\ 1 & 7 & 2 \\ 1 & 8 & 3 \end{bmatrix}. \tag{3.2}$$

Recent methodological work suggests exciting possibilities for modeling change that occurs in discrete segments. Cudeck and Klebe (2002) describe *multiphase models* for longitudinal data within the multilevel modeling framework. Multiphase regression models can be used to model change in multiple growth periods, each characterized by different functional forms (e.g., a downward linear slope followed immediately by an upward linear slope). The point of transition from one period (or *regime*) to another is known as a *change point* or *knot*. In theory, these change points may be modeled as aspects of change in their own right—as fixed parameters, estimated parameters, or random coefficients. For example, Cudeck and Klebe model the sharp quadratic growth, and subsequent gradual linear decline, in nonverbal intelligence across the life span. They estimated the age of transition from the first phase to the second phase as a random coefficient with a mean of 18.5 years and a Level 2 variance of 9.25.

Specifying multiphase models in the LGM framework is not always possible, but the ability to examine model fit, use aspects of change as predictor variables, and assess multiphase change in latent variables makes it a worthwhile topic to explore. Multiphase models with known change points may be examined by using partitioned Λ_y matrices, with each partition containing the basis curves for the corresponding segment of the trajectory. For example, the Λ_y matrix in Equation 3.3 represents a model for equally spaced occasions with an intercept and linear slope in the first segment (with means α_1 and α_2), a different intercept and linear slope in the second segment (with means α_3 and α_4), and a change point where *time* = 2.3. Alternatively, an unknown change point ω may be estimated as a function of model parameters when the Λ_y matrix is specified as in Equation 3.4, in which the time metric picks up in the fourth column where it left off in the second. Assuming that the segments ($\alpha_1 + \alpha_2 time$) and ($\alpha_3 + \alpha_4 time$) are continuous at *time* = ω, the values implied for y by both segments of the multiphase trajectory must be equal at ω. One of the parameters (say, α_3) is therefore redundant and can be eliminated by constraining it to equal a function of the other parameters, $\alpha_3 = \alpha_1 + (\alpha_2 - \alpha_4)\omega$, and estimating ω as a parameter. Similar algebra may be used in growth models with more complicated growth functions in multiple segments. There is currently no straightforward way to model change points as random coefficients in the LGM framework, although this can be done with multilevel modeling (see Cudeck & Klebe, 2002).

$$\Lambda_y = \begin{bmatrix} 1 & 0 & 0 & 0 \\ 1 & 1 & 0 & 0 \\ 1 & 2 & 0 & 0 \\ 0 & 0 & 1 & 0.7 \\ 0 & 0 & 1 & 1.7 \\ 0 & 0 & 1 & 2.7 \end{bmatrix}, \tag{3.3}$$

$$\Lambda_y = \begin{bmatrix} 1 & 0 & 0 & 0 \\ 1 & 1 & 0 & 0 \\ 1 & 2 & 0 & 0 \\ 0 & 0 & 1 & 3 \\ 0 & 0 & 1 & 4 \\ 0 & 0 & 1 & 5 \end{bmatrix}. \tag{3.4}$$

Modeling Change in Latent Variables With Multiple Indicators

None of the models presented earlier takes full advantage of one of the most basic and useful features of SEM—the ability to model relationships among latent variables with multiple measured indicators. Up to this point, we have said nothing about reliability or measurement error, but in fact, it is rare to encounter variables with near-perfect reliability in the social sciences. Routine applications of SEM explicitly model unreliability by partitioning observed variability into common variance (variance shared by a group of measured variables) and unique variance (a combination of measurement error and reliable variance specific to a variable). In most SEM applications, the diagonal elements of Θ_ε represent unique variance, but in LGM, the diagonal elements of Θ_ε represent a combination of measurement error and departure from the mean trend at each measurement occasion. To separate common from unique variance, repeated measures may be represented by latent variables and multiple time-specific indicators may be directly incorporated in the model.

These models are sometimes known as *curve-of-factors models* (S. C. Duncan & Duncan, 1996; McArdle, 1988), *latent variable longitudinal curve models* (Tisak & Meredith, 1990), or *second-order latent growth models* (Hancock, Kuo, & Lawrence, 2001; Hancock & Lawrence, 2006; Sayer & Cumsille, 2001); the repeated-measure latent variables are termed *first-order factors* and the growth factors (i.e., intercept and slope) are termed *second-order factors*. An example is presented in Figure 3.1.

Several advantages accrue by using latent repeated measures when multiple indicators are available. First, the second-order LGM explicitly recognizes the presence of measurement error in the repeated measures and models growth using latent variables adjusted for the presence of this error. Second, second-order growth curve models allow the separation of disturbance variation due to departure from the mean trend (temporal instability, reflected by $\psi_{33}-\psi_{66}$ in Figure 3.1) and unique variation due to measurement error (unreliability, reflected by Θ_{ε} in Figure 3.1). Third, second-order growth curve models permit tests of longitudinal factorial invariance, or *stationarity* (Sayer & Cumsille, 2001; Tisak & Meredith, 1990). It is extremely important that the latent variable of interest retain its meaning throughout the period of measurement (Willett, 1989). For this assumption to be supported, the factor structure should be invariant over repeated occasions (Chan, 1998; Meredith & Horn, 2001). That is, at the very least, factor loadings for similar items should be the same over repeated measures. Although it is beyond the scope of this book to delve into issues surrounding longitudinal factorial invariance, we cannot overemphasize its importance for studies of growth over time. For more details on specifying second-order growth curve models, consult Chan (1998), Hancock et al. (2001), and Sayer and Cumsille (2001).

Structured Latent Curves

The polynomial growth functions considered earlier are characterized by a property known as *dynamic consistency*. Loosely, dynamic consistency refers to the property that the "average of the curves" follows the same functional form as the "curve of the averages" (Singer & Willett, 2003). This property holds for linear growth, quadratic growth, and indeed any growth function that consists of a weighted linear composite of functions of time. A convenient consequence of dynamic consistency is that the first derivatives of the growth function with respect to growth parameters (if expressed in traditional polynomial form) are simply numbers, which can be coded directly into the Λ_y matrix using virtually any SEM software application. But growth functions in LGM need not be limited to the polynomial curves suggested by Meredith and Tisak (1990).

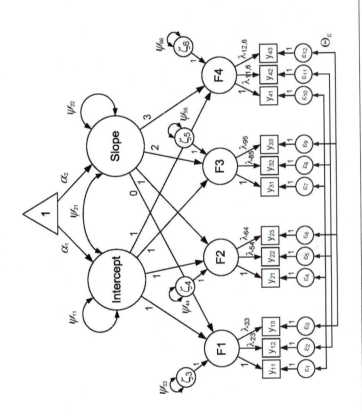

Figure 3.1   A Second-Order Growth Curve Model, Representing Linear Change in Four Repeated Measures of a Latent Variable With Three Measured Indicators.

NOTE: Included in the model, but not pictured, are paths (τ_y parameters) from the Triangle Constant 1 to the measured indicators not serving as scaling indicators (see Hancock et al., 2001). We chose to allow the unique factors of similar indicators to covary across repeated measures to acknowledge that covariances among indicators measured at different occasions are not expected to be completely explained by mutual reliance on growth factors.

63

Browne and du Toit (1991) and Browne (1993) propose and illustrate a *structured latent curve* (SLC) approach to modeling nonlinear growth functions not characterized by dynamic consistency. In SLC models, the loadings in Λ_y may assume values consistent with any hypothesized growth function $f(t, \theta)$ (a function of time, t, and growth parameters, θ), referred to as the *target function* (Blozis, 2004). The function $f(t, \theta)$ is assumed to be smooth and differentiable with respect to elements of θ. The SLC method of specifying growth models is a direct extension of Rao's (1958) EFA method of obtaining parameters for growth functions. The elements of Λ_y are not specified as fixed values. Rather, they are estimated, but are required to conform to basis curves consistent with $f(t, \theta)$. The polynomial curves considered in previous examples are special cases of this more general framework.

To understand the SLC framework, it is helpful to recognize that the loadings specified in the Λ_y matrix for polynomial growth curve models correspond to the first partial derivatives of the hypothesized growth function with respect to each growth parameter. For example, for the quadratic growth curve specified in Model 10, the target function is

$$\hat{y}_{it} = \theta_1 + \theta_2 t_{it} + \theta_3 t_{it}^2; \quad t = \{0, 2, 3, 4, 5\}. \tag{3.5}$$

The first derivatives of this function with respect to each growth parameter are, respectively,

$$\frac{\partial \hat{y}_{it}}{\partial \theta_1} = 1, \tag{3.6}$$

$$\frac{\partial \hat{y}_{it}}{\partial \theta_2} = t, \tag{3.7}$$

and

$$\frac{\partial \hat{y}_{it}}{\partial \theta_3} = t^2, \tag{3.8}$$

which are known quantities. Thus,

$$\Lambda_y = \begin{bmatrix} 1 & 0 & 0 \\ 1 & 2 & 4 \\ 1 & 3 & 9 \\ 1 & 4 & 16 \\ 1 & 5 & 25 \end{bmatrix}. \tag{3.9}$$

More complex—but dynamically inconsistent—growth functions, such as exponential, Gompertz, and logistic curves, may be specified in a similar manner. For growth functions that are not dynamically consistent, the growth parameters in θ may not reduce to simple functions of t, and may instead require more complicated specifications of Λ_y. For example, consider exponential growth. If an exponential process were appropriate for the mother–child closeness data (it is not, but let us pretend), the target function would be

$$\hat{y}_{it} = \theta_1 - (\theta_1 - \theta_2)e^{(1-t_{it})\theta_3}; \quad t = \{1, 3, 4, 5, 6\}. \tag{3.10}$$

The first derivatives of this function with respect to each growth parameter are, respectively,

$$\frac{\partial \hat{y}_{it}}{\partial \theta_1} = 1 - e^{\theta_3(1-t_{it})}, \tag{3.11}$$

$$\frac{\partial \hat{y}_{it}}{\partial \theta_2} = e^{\theta_3(1-t_{it})}, \tag{3.12}$$

and

$$\frac{\partial \hat{y}_{it}}{\partial \theta_3} = (\theta_1 - \theta_2)(t_{it} - 1)e^{\theta_3(1-t_{it})}. \tag{3.13}$$

Thus, if we let the initial occasion $t_{it} = 1$,

$$\Lambda_y = \begin{bmatrix} 0 & 1 & 0 \\ 1 - e^{-2\theta_3} & e^{-2\theta_3} & 2(\theta_1 - \theta_2)e^{-2\theta_3} \\ 1 - e^{-3\theta_3} & e^{-3\theta_3} & 3(\theta_1 - \theta_2)e^{-3\theta_3} \\ 1 - e^{-4\theta_3} & e^{-4\theta_3} & 4(\theta_1 - \theta_2)e^{-4\theta_3} \\ 1 - e^{-5\theta_3} & e^{-5\theta_3} & 5(\theta_1 - \theta_2)e^{-5\theta_3} \end{bmatrix}. \tag{3.14}$$

For polynomial curves, θ_1, θ_2, and θ_3 are estimated as means of three basis curve factors. In the exponential SLC, however, θ_1 and θ_2 are estimated as means but θ_3 is estimated using LISREL's additional parameter feature. Detailed treatments of this kind of model are presented in Browne (1993) and Blozis (2004). Blozis (2006) extends this method to model nonlinear trends in latent variables measured with multiple indicators, and Blozis (2007) extends the method to explore multivariate nonlinear change. Specialized software (e.g., AUFIT; du Toit & Browne, 1992) is required to estimate most SLC models, but LISREL can be used to estimate many such models using complex equality constraints.

Autoregressive Latent Trajectory Models

Although LGM is a useful and flexible approach for investigating change over time, there are alternative SEM-based strategies. One alternative model is the *autoregressive* or *Markov simplex* model proposed by Guttman (1954), in which each repeated measure is regarded as a function of the preceding measure and a time-specific disturbance term. Unlike the traditional LGM, the simplex model is not concerned with trends in the mean structure over time, but rather with explaining variance at each wave of measurement using the previous wave. Curran and Bollen (2001) and Bollen and Curran (2004, 2006) propose the *autoregressive latent trajectory* (ALT) model that combines features of both the LGM and simplex models. One example of an ALT model is depicted in Figure 3.2. The ALT model differs from the standard LGM model in two main respects. First, in the pictured parameterization of the ALT model, there is no disturbance term associated with the first repeated measure. Second, like the autoregressive or simplex model, directional paths (the ρ parameters in Figure 3.2) are specified to link adjacent repeated measures. It is common practice in specifying both the simplex model and ALT models to constrain the $\rho_{t,t-1}$ parameters to equality, although this constraint is by no means necessary. The ALT model is related to one of the TVC models presented earlier (Model 9; see Table 2.12), in which the value of the outcome variable at time $t-1$ is used as a predictor of the outcome at time t. Applications of univariate and multivariate ALT models can be found in Rodebaugh, Curran, and Chambless (2002) and Hussong, Hicks, Levy, and Curran (2001). A closely related model is the *latent difference score* model (McArdle, 2001; McArdle & Hamagami, 2001).

Categorical and Ordinal Outcomes

Our discussion so far has assumed that the repeated-measures possess interval or ratio characteristics. However, many variables in the social sciences are more properly treated as ordinal. It is difficult to conclude, for example, that dichotomous items or Likert-type scales with only three or four choices have interval properties (although with a sufficient number of choices, many rating scales may be treated as if they were continuous). When the repeated observed variable is ordinal, the data consist not of means and covariances but rather a potentially large contingency table, with each cell containing the number of respondents matching a particular response pattern. If the ordinal data can be assumed to reflect an underlying normally distributed latent variable, a multistage estimation procedure may be used

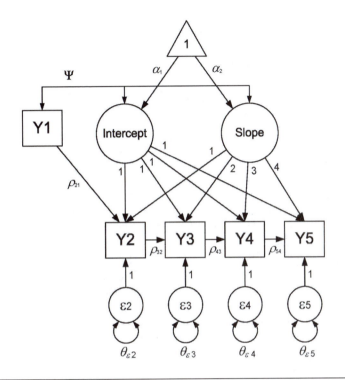

Figure 3.2   An Autoregressive Latent Trajectory Model for Five Repeated Measures.

to model growth (Mehta, Neale, & Flay, 2004). This procedure assumes that unobserved thresholds on the latent distribution at each occasion determine the multivariate probabilities associated with all response patterns. In the first stage, a link function is specified to model the multivariate ordinal response probabilities and a likelihood function is estimated for each case. In the second stage, a common measurement scale is established for the unobserved latent response variates, which are assumed to be normally distributed. Response thresholds are assumed to remain invariant over time. In the third stage, a growth model is fit to the scaled latent response variables. Currently, only a few software programs are capable of estimating such models, for example, Mplus and Mx. If some data are missing, Mx is the only option currently available. Jöreskog (2002) describes a similar procedure using LISREL, which involves fitting the model to a polychoric covariance matrix and means estimated from raw ordinal data.

The application of LGM to categorical data is receiving much attention in the methodological literature. For example, Liu and Powers (2007) recently described a method to model zero-inflated count data within the LGM framework. Many interesting advances are expected to occur in the foreseeable future. For more detail on methods for estimating growth models using binary or ordinal data, see Jöreskog (2002), Mehta et al. (2004), and B. Muthén and Asparouhov (2002).

Modeling Causal Effects Among Aspects of Change

To this point, intercept and slope (co)variances have been "unstructured" in the sense that they have been permitted to freely covary. We may instead elect to estimate directional effects among aspects of change; that is, we can model aspects of change as functions of other aspects of change. For example, if the time metric is centered at the final occasion of measurement, it may be of interest to model "endpoint" as a function of rate of change by regressing the intercept factor onto the slope factor. Alternatively, we could elect to center time at the initial occasion and model slopes as a linear function of intercepts. Caution is warranted here, however. Causes must logically precede effects, so it would be causally inconsistent to regress slopes on intercepts unless the time origin occurs at or before the initial measurement.

Muthén and Curran (1997) creatively capitalize on this feature of SEM to model treatment effects in situations where participants are randomly assigned to (at least) two groups and repeatedly measured on some outcome of interest, such as in intervention studies. They suggest fitting the same growth curve to both groups, constraining the linear growth parameters to equality across groups (see Figure 3.3). A second slope factor (Tx Slope) is added to the model for the experimental group. The control group thus provides a baseline trajectory against which the experimental group's trajectory may be compared. Any additional change observed beyond that associated with the first slope factor is due to the treatment effect. An important aspect of their model is that the additional treatment slope factor may be regressed on the intercept factor (initial status), allowing the examination of an intercept × treatment interaction. For example, it may be the case that mother–child pairs with relatively low initial closeness may benefit more over time from an intervention targeting the prevention of externalizing behaviors. In Muthén and Curran's model, the intercept factor would influence a third latent variable (intervention), which in turn would affect the measured variable across time, but only in the experimental group.

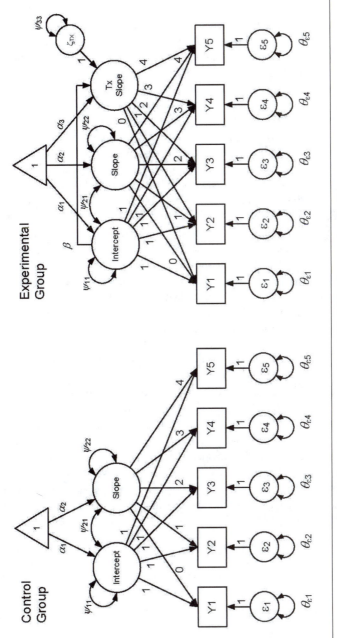

Figure 3.3 Muthén and Curran's (1997) Two-Group Growth Model for Intervention Studies.

Summary

In this chapter, we have described several specialized extensions of LGM that demonstrate its generality and flexibility as an analytic tool. It is possible to combine features of the models discussed here and to expand these models in other ways, depending on the researcher's requirements. For example, it is feasible to explore growth mixture models applied to cohort-sequential data and to examine the effects of TVCs or exogenous predictors in parallel process ALT models (Bollen & Curran, 2004; Curran & Willoughby, 2003). Simons-Morton, Chen, Abroms, and Haynie (2004) model three parallel processes (adolescent smoking, friend smoking, and parental involvement), including time-invariant predictors and specifying effects of intercepts on slopes both within and between processes. Sayer and Willett (1998) combine piecewise and parallel process growth models, fitting them simultaneously in two groups. McArdle (1989) describes a multiple-groups parallel process model. Finally, we did not present an example of this kind of model, but it is straightforward to treat intercepts and slopes as predictors of outcome variables. For example, it might be important to test the hypothesis that rate of acquisition of a skill predicts individual differences in ability years later. Muthén and Curran (1997) present some models in which intercept and slope factors are used to predict a distal outcome or to predict intercept and slope factors associated with a different repeated-measures variable.

The LGM framework permits specification and testing of several kinds of interaction or moderation hypotheses. For example, researchers can test hypotheses about the interaction among two or more exogenous predictors of slope (Curran et al., 2004; Li, Duncan, & Acock, 2000; Preacher et al., 2006), between initial status and time in determining an outcome (Muthén & Curran, 1997), or between time and a TVC (see discussion of Model 9 in Chapter 2). LGM can be extended to three (or more) levels of hierarchically organized data by employing multilevel SEM (Mehta & Neale, 2005; B. Muthén, 1997). At the other end of the spectrum, it is also possible to fit simple ANOVA, MANOVA, and simplex models in LGM as special cases (Meredith & Tisak, 1990).

CHAPTER 4. RELATIONSHIPS
BETWEEN LGM AND MULTILEVEL MODELING

A powerful alternative to LGM for modeling longitudinal data is multilevel modeling (MLM; Bryk & Raudenbush, 1987, 1992; Goldstein, 1995; Hox, 2002; Kreft & de Leeuw, 1998; Raudenbush & Bryk, 2002). Multilevel models, also known as *hierarchical linear models* (HLMs; Bryk & Raudenbush, 1992; Raudenbush & Bryk, 2002), *mixed models*, *variance component models*, or *random coefficient models*, allow hierarchical partitioning of variance, an important ability when analyzing hierarchically nested data, such as data in which students are nested within schools. Gentle introductions to MLM can be found in Hofmann (1997), Kreft and de Leeuw (1998), and Luke (2004). MLM and LGM stem from different traditions of research and statistical theory, and each has developed its own terminology and standard ways of framing research questions. However, it has become clear that there exists much overlap between the two methodologies under some circumstances. In this section, we explore this overlap.

In hierarchically nested data, the lowest level of the hierarchy is referred to as Level 1, with successively higher levels receiving larger numbers. Nested data are found in many settings: They can consist, for example, of students (Level 1) nested within schools (Level 2), workers within industry, or clients in therapy groups. Outcome variables are measured at Level 1, and their predictors can be measured at Level 1, Level 2, or higher levels. Typically, each group (Level 2 unit) will show different relationships between explanatory variables and outcome measures. These different within-group relationships can often be explained using predictor variables that vary systematically between groups. For example, students from private schools may show higher test scores than students from public schools, and a researcher may wish to test the utility of different interventions to close this gap. In this case, MLM could be used to investigate the possibly differential effect of a remedial reading program in each of these settings.

MLM for Repeated-Measures Data

There is a straightforward conceptual link between using MLM to study nesting within groups and to study growth curves (Diggle, Liang, & Zeger, 1994; Longford, 1993). In repeated-measures designs, occasions of measurement (Level 1) are nested within individuals (Level 2). Once it is recognized that measurement occasions can be thought of as Level 1 units hierarchically nested within Level 2 units, MLM analysis of longitudinal data proceeds much as would any application of MLM.

A researcher typically begins by estimating a *random-effects ANOVA* model—a no-predictor model in which only the nested structure of the data is taken into account—to determine whether or not anything would be gained by using MLM over the more traditional ordinary least squares approach. This model partitions variance in the outcome measure into that portion associated with time (variance *within* individuals over repeated measurement occasions, Level 1) and that portion associated with individual-level differences (variance *between* individuals, Level 2). If there is a significant amount of Level 2 variation to be explained, analysis typically proceeds in small steps by adding predictor variables to the equation. This procedure allows for change in the outcome variable to be defined over the Level 1 variable *time*, and for this change to be further modeled by including Level 2 predictors that vary between individuals.

These predictors can have either fixed or random coefficients. Fixed coefficients are coefficients that ignore variability in their estimates associated with Level 2 units. For instance, if a researcher were interested in modeling the effect of child's weekly allowance (Level 2) on a child's math performance over time (Level 1), specifying income as a fixed coefficient would yield the overall, average effect of allowance on math performance. Specifying the slope coefficient of allowance as random, however, would additionally yield an estimate of the between-child variability in the effects of allowance on math performance, and this estimate of between-child variability in turn could be modeled by other predictors. Among several benefits, random coefficients have the advantage that the variance in their estimates can be predicted by explanatory variables at higher levels of analysis. Typically in MLM, these predictors are first included with fixed regression coefficients and then, if model fit can be significantly improved, with random coefficients.

A significant advantage of using the MLM approach to examine repeated-measures data is its ability to use all available data, even for individuals with missing data on some occasions, assuming the missing data are MAR. Additionally, with MLM it is unnecessary to assume that every subject is measured at the same time points or ages, or even the same number of occasions. Considering these benefits, it would seem that for researchers desiring reliable results and a flexible analysis model in the context of a repeated-measures study, MLM has much to offer.

Model Specification

Typically, an MLM for the analysis of linear change represents the outcome, y, as a linear function of time[1]:

$$y_{ij} = \underline{\beta}_{0j} + \underline{\beta}_{1j}(time_{ij}) + \varepsilon_{ij}, \tag{4.1}$$

$$\varepsilon_{ij} \sim N\{0, \sigma_\varepsilon^2\}, \tag{4.2}$$

where $\underline{\beta}_{0j}$ is the intercept for individual j, $\underline{\beta}_{1j}$ is the slope for individual j, and ε_{ij} is the residual for individual j at occasion i (normally distributed with mean zero and homoskedastic variance σ_ε^2). Both intercept and slope are typically treated as random variables, and their between-individual variance is modeled as follows:

$$\underline{\beta}_{0j} = \gamma_{00} + u_{0j}, \tag{4.3}$$

$$\underline{\beta}_{1j} = \gamma_{10} + u_{1j}, \tag{4.4}$$

$$\begin{bmatrix} u_{0j} \\ u_{1j} \end{bmatrix} \sim N\left\{ \begin{bmatrix} 0 \\ 0 \end{bmatrix}, \begin{bmatrix} \tau_{00} & \\ \tau_{10} & \tau_{11} \end{bmatrix} \right\}. \tag{4.5}$$

In specifying them as random, both intercept ($\underline{\beta}_{0j}$) and slope ($\underline{\beta}_{1j}$) terms are modeled as functions of a fixed, average effect characterizing all individuals in the sample, plus each individual's deviation from that fixed effect. The u terms in Equations 4.3 and 4.4 represent these deviations (u_{0j} for intercept, and u_{1j} for slope, respectively). The variances and covariance of these deviations (τ_{00}, τ_{11}, and τ_{10}) are often of theoretical interest, for instance, when a researcher wants to know whether children who have an initially higher math ability also improve more quickly than those with lower initial ability. A positive covariance between math intercept and slope would suggest that those with initially higher math ability also improve more quickly over time than did those with lower initial ability. Combining Equations 4.1, 4.3, and 4.4 yields an expanded equation:

$$y_{ij} = \gamma_{00} + \gamma_{10}(time_{ij}) + u_{0j} + u_{1j}(time_{ij}) + \varepsilon_{ij}. \tag{4.6}$$

Equation 4.6 presents the multilevel regression equation as the sum of a fixed component ($\gamma_{00} + \gamma_{10}(time_{ij})$) and a random portion ($u_{0j} + u_{1j}(time_{ij}) + \varepsilon_{ij}$). This model estimates two fixed effects (γ_{00} and γ_{10}) as well as four random effects—the variances and covariance of individuals' deviations from fixed estimates of intercept and slope (τ_{00}, τ_{11}, and τ_{10}), as well as any remaining variance not explained by the model (σ_{ε}^2). These estimates of the variances of intercept and slope, as well as the covariance of intercept and slope, allow for informed reasoning about the nature of the effects under study.

Although similar to traditional regression, MLM is more powerful in that the influence of interindividual and intraindividual factors can be separately estimated, as can the relationships (i.e., covariances) among aspects of change. This latter property is especially useful when MLM is applied to the study of multivariate change and when relationships between initial level (intercept) and rate of change (slope) are of interest. Of course, many special cases and extensions to this standard random intercept, random slope model are possible. For example, it is possible to investigate the effects of time-varying or time-invariant covariates, impose and test constraints on model parameters, and estimate multivariate models.

Parameter Estimation

ML or FIML estimation is usually used to obtain parameter estimates in MLM. As in SEM, ML estimation yields a set of parameter estimates under which, given the assumption of multivariate normality, the observed data may be regarded as most likely. Different software packages approach the problem of obtaining ML solutions in different ways. For example, MLwiN (Rasbash et al., 1999) uses an iterative generalized least squares algorithm to arrive at a ML solution for all parameters. Alternatively, when ML estimation is applied to the least squares residuals, the method is known as restricted maximum likelihood (REML). The algorithm used to obtain an REML solution in MLwiN is restricted iterative generalized least squares. In contrast to MLwiN, HLM (Bryk, Raudenbush, & Congdon, 1996) uses an expectation maximization algorithm to provide empirical Bayes estimates, which, when normality is assumed, are equivalent to generalized least squares estimates. FIML estimation includes both fixed and random parameters in the likelihood function, whereas REML estimates the variance components after the fixed effects have been removed from the model (Hox, 2000, 2002). Hox further points out that, because of this, REML should not be used for chi-square difference tests involving freeing constraints on fixed parameters (see also Singer & Willett, 2003, pp. 90, 118).

Model Evaluation

As with ordinary least squares regression, hypotheses in MLM are usually tested by assessing the statistical and practical significance of fixed regression coefficients, although the variances and covariances of random coefficients are often of interest as well. An informal test of the significance of a parameter is conducted by dividing the point estimate by its standard error; if the ratio exceeds about 2.00 (1.96 in an infinite sample), the parameter estimate is said to be significantly different from zero at the .05 significance level. See Hox (1998) for a more thorough discussion of significance testing in MLM.

Information on overall model fit in MLM is also available, and reported as a *deviance statistic*, defined as $-2\ln L$, where L is the value of the likelihood function at convergence (Hox, 2002; Kreft & de Leeuw, 1998; Li, Duncan, Harmer, Acock, & Stoolmiller, 1998). Alone, the deviance statistic does not provide an easily interpretable measure of the fit of the overall model because it is highly dependent on sample size. However, differences between deviance statistics from nested models are distributed as χ^2 with degrees of freedom equal to the difference in the number of parameters between the nested models (Goldstein, 1995; Hox, 2000, 2002; Li et al., 1998).

Areas of Overlap Between MLM and LGM

Both MLM and LGM may be used in many of the same situations involving repeated-measures data; indeed, for a large subset of models, the two approaches yield identical results owing to identical model expressions at the equation level. It is not new to suggest that MLM and LGM are similar— in fact, various aspects of overlap between the two approaches have been repeatedly demonstrated in the literature. Equivalent repeated-measures models may be specified within each framework such that identical parameter estimates are obtained (within rounding error) (Bauer, 2003; Bauer & Curran, 2002; Chou, Bentler, & Pentz, 1998; Curran, 2003; Hox, 2000, 2002; Khoo & Muthén, 2000; Li et al., 1998; MacCallum & Kim, 2000; MacCallum et al., 1997; Raudenbush, 2001; Rovine & Molenaar, 2000; Stoel, 2003; Wendorf, 2002; Willett & Sayer, 1994). For example, in the case of the basic linear growth model already described, all six parameters of interest in the MLM representation have equivalent parameters in LGM representation. Specifically, the mean intercept estimates are represented by γ_{00} and α_1 for the MLM and LGM approaches, respectively (see Table 4.1). Likewise, mean change over time, the slope parameter, is represented by γ_{10} in MLM and α_2 in LGM. The variances and covariance of the intercept and the slope and the disturbance variance are also represented in both approaches. Even though the computational algorithms employed in SEM are different from those used in MLM, they are all intended to yield ML estimates of parameters (and their standard errors) using as much information as possible. Consequently, for models having an equivalent representation in the two frameworks, it is reasonable to expect parameter estimates obtained within the MLM paradigm to be identical to corresponding parameter estimates obtained within the LGM paradigm.[2] Table 4.1 contains a brief demonstration of this phenomenon using the mother–child closeness data and Model 4. The multilevel analysis was conducted using MLwiN 1.1; the parameter estimates and *SE*s are identical to those reported in Table 2.6.

It is worth noting another interesting parallel between MLM and LGM. In the MLM tradition, it is common practice to obtain *empirical Bayes estimates* of the random coefficients, model-based estimates of intercepts and slopes for each Level 2 unit, usually for plotting or diagnostic purposes. These estimates are also called *posterior means*, so called because they are the estimated means of the posterior distribution of the random coefficients given the data, or *shrinkage estimates*, because they are "shrunken" toward the intercept and slope means to a degree proportional to each Level 2 unit's reliability. In the latent variable tradition, empirical Bayes estimates are equivalent to *factor scores*, posterior estimates of latent variables. In LGM, these estimates are model-implied values of intercepts and slopes, weighted by the reliability of each individual's (or Level 2 unit's) contribution. We regard computation of factor scores as of little practical value in LGM, mainly because they are biased estimates that do not accurately reflect individual trajectories. Furthermore, Bartholomew (2007) points out that it is impossible to assign factor scores to individual cases with any certainty

TABLE 4.1

Parameter Estimates for the
Multilevel Model Corresponding to Model 4

MLM	LGM	Interpretation	Estimate
$\hat{\gamma}_{00}$	$\hat{\alpha}_1$	Mean intercept	38.00 (0.08)
$\hat{\gamma}_{10}$	$\hat{\alpha}_2$	Mean slope	−0.36 (0.02)
$\hat{\tau}_{00}$	$\hat{\psi}_{11}$	Intercept variance	2.98 (0.29)
$\hat{\tau}_{11}$	$\hat{\psi}_{22}$	Slope variance	0.14 (0.02)
$\hat{\tau}_{10}$	$\hat{\psi}_{21}$	Intercept–slope covariance	0.25 (0.06)
$\hat{\sigma}_\varepsilon^2$	$\hat{\theta}_\varepsilon$	Disturbance variance	3.70 (0.10)

NOTE: Numbers in parentheses are standard errors of parameter estimates.

MLM = Multilevel modeling; LGM = Latent growth curve modeling.

because the model implies a distribution of such scores for each individual. Factor scores represent the means of these distributions.

Areas of Differentiation Between MLM and LGM

For the class of longitudinal data considered here, LGM and MLM are mathematically equivalent. At least some of the perceived differences between the approaches are due to differences in the software designed to implement them (Raudenbush & Bryk, 2002) and historical tradition. Whereas it is still true that each type of analysis has flexibility limitations with respect to the other, it is also true that many previous limitations have recently vanished in the wake of improvements to software. Our goal in the previous section was to illustrate the overlap between the MLM and LGM paradigms for longitudinal data analysis. However, there are also applications of these models that are possible in one framework and not the other. Some of this lack of overlap in methods is due to limitations in current software designed to implement them. For example, a clear advantage of LGM over MLM is the ability to specify a measurement model in LGM. That is, the repeatedly measured variable need not be free of measurement error, as is assumed in MLM. Within the LGM framework, each repeated measure may be specified as a latent variable with multiple indicators (Curran, 2000; Khoo & Muthén, 2000). Assuming the factor structure of the repeatedly assessed latent variable does not change over time, such a model has potentially large statistical power advantages over the corresponding measured-variable model. There is theoretically nothing preventing such modeling options from being incorporated into MLM software packages, and indeed Mplus can estimate multilevel structural equation models (L. K. Muthén & Muthén, 1998–2006).

A second limitation of MLM software is that it does not allow model parameters to serve as predictors of other variables in the system. The LGM approach, by viewing these aspects of change not as parameters but as variables in their own right, does not suffer from this shortcoming (Bauer & Curran, 2002; Hox, 2000). In fact, many complex models that are currently difficult or impossible to specify in MLM may be specified easily in LGM. An example from recent literature is the LGM approach to testing hypotheses of group differences in change over time introduced by B. O. Muthén and Curran (1997) and discussed in Chapter 3. At present, no purely MLM program can estimate a model in which one latent construct influences another as in the Muthén and Curran model.

A third limitation of the MLM approach to modeling change concerns LGM's capability of estimating factor loadings, a useful feature in both unspecified growth models (Model 11 in Chapter 2) and SLC models. In the MLM framework, time is treated as a variable whose values are known (MacCallum et al., 1997).

Although LGM has some advantages that are uniquely its own, MLM is not without its own advantages. A clear advantage of MLM over LGM is MLM's ability to accommodate more than two hierarchical levels. For example, consider a data set consisting of repeated measures nested within students, who in turn are nested within classrooms. Specification of such a model would be straightforward within the MLM framework but very difficult to specify using LGM (although it is possible; Curran, 2003; Muthén & Muthén, 1998–2006). For good overviews of multilevel structural equation models, see Hox (2000) and Mehta and Neale (2005). In addition, whereas the SLC model serves as a close approximation to complex nonlinear functions of time, such functions often can be directly represented in the MLM framework without the need for approximation, depending on the software package used.

We have tried to outline in this section some of the differences governing model specification that currently exist between MLM and LGM approaches. If we were to expand our focus somewhat, we could have addressed a number of other issues. Some of these include historically rooted differences, such as differences in the use or nonuse of model fit statistics for the corresponding models we describe or differences in how model modification indices are often seen as capitalizing on chance in LGM/SEM (MacCallum, Roznowski, & Necowitz, 1992), but how freeing parameters in MLM is deemed acceptable and even encouraged. In addition to noting that historical factors determine in large part what researchers consider acceptable practice in these traditionally distinct approaches, we note that some supposed advantages of one technique over the other are functions of analytic traditions impacting software development, not necessarily advantages of one technique over the other.

Although they emerged from different theoretical and practical origins, MLM and LGM are both useful tools for the behavioral researcher and can provide answers to similar questions about change over time. Owing to recent developments in software and estimation techniques, models previously considered impossible in one method or the other are now possible. For example, missing-data algorithms have allowed LGM approaches to more closely match MLM applications. Additionally, MLM software now has the capability to model alternative error structures, previously noted as a strength of LGM. The discrepancies between MLM and LGM are rapidly disappearing, but the methods are currently still distinct enough to warrant careful consideration of which approach to use for model testing and development. We expect that eventually the distinctions between LGM and MLM may disappear altogether with advances in model specification frameworks and software.

Software

A number of software packages exist for conducting MLM. Dedicated applications include aML, HLM, and MLwiN. Several general statistical packages (R, SAS, Splus, SPSS, Stata, and SYSTAT) and SEM programs (EQS, LISREL, and Mplus) now include the ability to estimate multilevel models. Of these, R, SAS, Splus, and Stata contain routines to estimate nonlinear multilevel models. Models for binary and ordinal responses require estimation methods other than the standard REML or FIML methods (e.g., maximum marginal likelihood, penalized quasi likelihood, empirical Bayes, or Markov chain Monte Carlo), so specialized software is generally required for these data types. aML, freely available online, can flexibly handle several nonstandard data types and models, including truncated or censored regression, multilevel hazard models, ordinal or count data, splines, and many others. MIX, a collection of standalone programs or macros for SPSS and SAS, can estimate multilevel models with many different data types. For researchers wanting to model growth in ordinal, count, or generally nonnormal data, we recommend investigating some of these alternatives to LGM. More information about software for multilevel models can be found in de Leeuw and Kreft (2001) and Snijders and Bosker (1999), as well as in user's guides to the software applications mentioned above.

Notes

1. Our notation, which matches that of Kreft and de Leeuw (1998), denotes random coefficients with underscores. In the matrix representation of latent growth curves discussed earlier, underscores denoted vectors.

2. One demonstration of this close correspondence is provided by Hox (2000), who found that parameter estimates are more similar across methods to the degree that missing data are MCAR versus MAR.

CHAPTER 5. SUMMARY

In this book, we have provided an introduction to latent growth curve modeling, illustrated many potential applications with data, and described several extensions and advanced applications that lie outside the basic LGM framework. We demonstrated how models more advanced than simple linear models may be specified and evaluated, including variations using group as a predictor, related growth curves, and cohort-sequential designs. The variety of possible models we demonstrate shows that this family of techniques is both flexible and powerful. LGM is an area of applied statistics receiving much attention in recent methodological literature, and advances are rapidly accumulating. This book provides a conceptual, theoretical, and applied basis for researchers seeking to orient themselves in this quickly advancing area.

One of the most attractive qualities of the LGM framework is the potential for extending existing methods in new ways. In particular, we feel that the structured latent curve approach has strong potential for use in applied settings. The only impediment to applying complex growth curve models in practice is the lack of widely available, user-friendly software, a problem that will doubtless be remedied in the future. Work is also progressing rapidly on a variety of related topics, including growth curve models with latent interaction terms (Li et al., 2000), plotting and probing simple effects in conditional growth curves (Curran et al., 2004; Preacher et al., 2006), and the further development and refinement of growth mixture models (Bauer & Curran, 2003a, 2003b, 2004). In addition, much recent work has been devoted to treatment of missing data and categorical outcomes. Opportunities for extending LGM exist in other areas as well. For example, even though the disturbance terms in ε are usually specified to be independent, this constraint is not necessary (Browne, 1993; McArdle, 1988). It is common to permit the disturbances to follow a first-order autoregressive structure, in which the covariances of adjacent disturbance terms are specified as free parameters (Browne, 1993; Meredith & Tisak, 1990; Willett & Sayer, 1994). It is also possible to specify a causal structure underlying error covariation.

Although we focus on LGM in the context of a frequentist approach to statistics, computing advances have made Bayesian approaches more useful than they once were for the applied researcher. A Bayesian approach to LGM embraces model fitting for ordered categorical and dichotomous variables, nonlinear growth models, multiple-sample and mixture models, models fit to ignorable or nonignorable missing data, models fit to nonnormal data, and combinations of these types of models that are often problematic in standard SEM. It is also possible to incorporate prior information during model estimation, a hallmark of Bayesian analysis. In short, a Bayesian approach to LGM is potentially flexible and powerful, but its use requires advanced knowledge. Interested readers are referred to Lee (2007); Scheines, Hoijtink, and Boomsma (1999); and Zhang, Hamagami, Wang, Nesselroade, and Grimm (2007) for information on these emerging techniques.

This book focuses on LGM, but LGM is not the only latent variable approach to investigating longitudinal data. Techniques related to LGM include exploratory longitudinal factor analysis (Tisak & Meredith, 1989, 1990) and the use of longitudinal SEM to investigate reliability, validity, and stability over time (Tisak & Tisak, 1996, 2000). Autoregressive models and autoregressive cross-lagged models are viable alternatives to growth curve models in many circumstances (see Bollen & Curran, 2004; Curran et al., 1997). Multilevel models, the topic of the preceding chapter, also have great utility for analyzing longitudinal data.

Although we have tried to cover the information necessary to achieve a good grasp of the basics of LGM, our treatment is far from exhaustive. Our purpose was to provide an overview of basic LGM methodology, illustrate its use, and describe some recent advances in methodological research. Beyond these central concerns, a broad take-home message is simply that a number of insights into the nature of data may be gained by formulating models that explicitly incorporate time (Collins, 2006). As Anderson (1993, p. 929) put it, "There is no substitute for a true longitudinal study." LGM analyses represent one family of approaches that can aid the researcher in formulating hypotheses and exploring the shapes and correlates of trends.

The Reference section is intentionally long, as a secondary goal of the book is to provide an entrée to the literature for the interested reader. For more information on specific topics covered in this book, we recommend consulting the cited articles. Good introductions to LGM are Byrne and Crombie (2003), Chan (1998), Curran (2000), Curran and Hussong (2003), Hancock and Lawrence (2006), and Willett and Sayer (1994). Singer and Willett (2003, chap 8) provide good introductions to both SEM and LGM. For more sophisticated and detailed treatments of SEM in general, we enthusiastically recommend Bollen (1989); for LGM specifically, we recommend Bollen and Curran (2006).

APPENDIX

Several online resources are available to researchers interested in learning more about latent growth curve modeling. We briefly outline a few such resources here.

Plotting and Probing Interactions in Latent Growth Curve Models

Interaction (moderation) effects in ordinary linear regression are commonly illustrated with interaction plots. Interaction plots represent the regression of Y on X at conditional values of some moderator M to facilitate understanding. One of the primary advantages of the LCA framework is that the factors representing intercept and slope can serve as endogenous (dependent) variables in other model equations, as in Model 6. When these aspects of change are predicted by some external variable M, the dependence of the repeated measures variable Y on time is conditional on M in much the same way that the regression of Y on X is conditional on M in ordinary regression. Conversely, we could claim with equal legitimacy that the dependence of Y on M is conditional on time. Such effects are termed *cross-level interactions.*

Methods commonly employed to illustrate interaction effects in regression (e.g., Aiken & West, 1991) can also be used in the LGM framework (Curran et al., 2004; Preacher et al., 2006). It is possible to plot the model-implied mean trajectory of Y over time at any conditional value of M. It is also possible to plot the regression of Y on M for any given occasion. Utilities for plotting cross-level interactions are available at http://www .quantpsy.org, along with a tutorial and a fully worked example.

Illustrating Individual Trajectories

Most information derived from an LGM analysis is summary information; results are usually in the form of mean trends and variability about those means, and individual cases tend to get lost in the shuffle. Carrig, Wirth, and Curran (2004) describe a SAS macro (OLS*traj*) that can be used to create plots of group-level or individual-level trajectories. OLS*traj* may be used either as a preliminary step to help plan a more involved LGM analysis or as a method to illustrate data. In addition to providing plots of individual trajectories, OLS*traj* can provide group-level histograms and box plots of parameter estimates and can export individual parameter estimates as data. OLS*traj* and an accompanying manual are available at http://www.unc.edu/~curran/olstraj.htm.

Syntax

All the LISREL, Mplus, and Mx syntax used for analyses in this book is available at the first author's Web site, http://www.quantpsy.org/.

REFERENCES

Aber, M. S., & McArdle, J. J. (1991). Latent growth curve approaches to modeling the development of competence. In M. Chandler & M. Chapman (Eds.), *Criteria for competence: Controversies in the conceptualization and assessment of children's abilities* (pp. 231–258). Hillsdale, NJ: Lawrence Erlbaum.

Aiken, L. S., & West, S. G. (1991). *Multiple regression: Testing and interpreting interactions.* Thousand Oaks, CA: Sage.

Allison, P. D. (1987). Estimation of linear models with incomplete data. In C. C. Clogg (Ed.), *Sociological methodology* (pp. 71–103). San Francisco: Jossey-Bass.

Allison, P. D. (2002). *Missing data.* Newbury Park, CA: Sage.

Anderson, E. R. (1993). Analyzing change in short-term longitudinal research using cohort-sequential designs. *Journal of Consulting and Clinical Psychology, 61,* 929–940.

Arbuckle, J. L. (1996). Full information estimation in the presence of incomplete data. In G. A. Marcoulides & R. E. Schumacker (Eds.), *Advanced structural equation modeling: Issues and techniques* (pp. 243–277). Mahwah, NJ: Lawrence Erlbaum.

Arbuckle, J., & Friendly, M. L. (1977). On rotating to smooth functions. *Psychometrika, 42,* 127–140.

Arbuckle, J. L., & Wothke, W. (1999). *AMOS 4.0 user's guide.* Chicago: SPSS, Inc.

Arminger, G., Wittenberg, J., & Schepers, A. (1996). *MECOSA 3 user guide.* Friedrichsdorf/Ts, Germany: ADDITIVE GmbH.

Baer, J., & Schmitz, M. F. (2000). Latent growth curve modeling with a cohort sequential design. *Social Work Research, 24,* 243–247.

Baker, G. A. (1954). Factor analysis of relative growth. *Growth, 18,* 137–143.

Bartholomew, D. J. (2007). Three faces of factor analysis. In R. Cudeck & R. C. MacCallum (Eds.), *Factor analysis at 100: Historical developments and future directions* (pp. 9–21). Mahwah, NJ: Lawrence Erlbaum.

Bauer, D. J. (2003). Estimating multilevel linear models as structural equation models. *Journal of Educational and Behavioral Statistics, 28,* 135–167.

Bauer, D. J. (2005, October). *Incongruence between the statistical theory and substantive application of growth mixture models in psychological research.* Cattell Award address presented at the annual meeting of the Society of Multivariate Experimental Psychology, Lake Tahoe, CA.

Bauer, D. J. (2007). Observations on the use of growth mixture models in psychological research. *Multivariate Behavioral Research, 42,* 757–786.

Bauer, D. J., & Curran, P. J. (2002, June). *Estimating multilevel linear models as structural equation models.* Paper presented at the meeting of the Psychometric Society, Chapel Hill, NC.

Bauer, D. J., & Curran, P. J. (2003a). Distributional assumptions of growth mixture models: Implications for overextraction of latent trajectory classes. *Psychological Methods, 8,* 338–363.

Bauer, D. J., & Curran, P. J. (2003b). Over-extracting latent trajectory classes: Much ado about nothing? Reply to Rindskopf (2003), Muthén (2003), and Cudeck and Henly (2003). *Psychological Methods, 8,* 384–393.

Bauer, D. J., & Curran, P. J. (2004). The integration of continuous and discrete latent variable models: Potential problems and promising opportunities. *Psychological Methods, 9,* 3–29.

Bell, R. Q. (1953). Convergence: An accelerated longitudinal approach. *Child Development, 24,* 145–152.

Bell, R. Q. (1954). An experimental test of the accelerated longitudinal approach. *Child Development, 25,* 281–286.

Bentler, P. M. (1995). *EQS structural equations program manual.* Encino, CA: Multivariate Software.

Bentler, P. M., & Bonett, D. G. (1980). Significance tests and goodness-of-fit in the analysis of covariance structures. *Psychological Bulletin, 88,* 588–606.

Biesanz, J. C., Deeb-Sossa, N., Papadakis, A. A., Bollen, K. A., & Curran, P. J. (2004). The role of coding time in estimating and interpreting growth curve models. *Psychological Methods, 9,* 30–52.

Bijleveld, C. C. J. H., & van der Kamp, L. J. T. (1998). *Longitudinal data analysis: Designs, models, and methods.* Newbury Park, CA: Sage.

Blackson, T. C., Tarter, R. E., Loeber, R., Ammerman, R. T., & Windle, M. (1996). The influence of paternal substance abuse and difficult temperament on sons' disengagement from family and deviant peers. *Journal of Youth and Adolescence, 25,* 389–411.

Blozis, S. A. (2004). Structured latent curve models for the study of change in multivariate repeated measures. *Psychological Methods, 9,* 334–353.

Blozis, S. A. (2006). A second-order structured latent curve model for longitudinal data. In K. van Montfort, H. Oud, & A. Satorra (Eds.), *Longitudinal models in the behavioral and related sciences.* Mahwah, NJ: Lawrence Erlbaum.

Blozis, S. A. (2007). On fitting nonlinear latent curve models to multiple variables measured longitudinally. *Structural Equation Modeling, 14,* 179–201.

Bock, R. D. (1979). Univariate and multivariate analysis of variance of time-structured data. In J. R. Nesselroade & P. B. Baltes (Eds.), *Longitudinal research in the study of behavior and development* (pp. 199–231). New York: Academic Press.

Bollen, K. A. (1989). *Structural equations with latent variables.* New York: Wiley.

Bollen, K. A., & Curran, P. J. (2004). Autoregressive latent trajectory (ALT) models: A synthesis of two traditions. *Sociological Methods & Research, 32,* 336–383.

Bollen, K. A., & Curran, P. J. (2006). *Latent curve models: A structural equation perspective.* Hoboken, NJ: Wiley.

Browne, M. W. (1993). Structured latent curve models. In C. M. Cuadras & C. R. Rao (Eds.), *Multivariate analysis: Future directions 2* (pp. 171–197). Amsterdam: Elsevier-North Holland.

Browne, M. W., & Cudeck, R. (1993). Alternative ways of assessing model fit. In K. A. Bollen & J. S. Long (Eds.), *Testing structural equation models* (pp. 136–162). Newbury Park, CA: Sage.

Browne, M. W., & du Toit, S. H. C. (1991). Models for learning data. In L. M. Collins & J. L. Horn (Eds.), *Best methods for the analysis of change* (pp. 47–68). Washington, DC: American Psychological Association.

Browne, M. W., MacCallum, R. C., Kim, C., Andersen, B. L., & Glaser, R. (2002). When fit indices and residuals are incompatible. *Psychological Methods, 7,* 403–421.

Bryk, A. S., & Raudenbush, S. W. (1987). Application of hierarchical linear models to assessing change. *Psychological Bulletin, 101,* 147–158.

Bryk, A. S., & Raudenbush, S. W. (1992). *Hierarchical linear models: Applications and data analysis methods.* Newbury Park, CA: Sage.

Bryk, A. S., Raudenbush, S. W., & Congdon, R. T. (1996). *HLM: Hierarchical linear and nonlinear modeling with the HLM/2L and HLM/3L programs.* Chicago: Scientific Software International.

Buist, K. L., Deković, M., Meeus, W., & van Aken, M. A. G. (2002). Developmental patterns in adolescent attachment to mother, father and sibling. *Journal of Youth and Adolescence, 31,* 167–176.

Byrne, B. M., & Crombie, G. (2003). Modeling and testing change: An introduction to the latent growth curve model. *Understanding Statistics, 2,* 177–203.

Carrig, M. M., Wirth, R. J., & Curran, P. J. (2004). A SAS macro for estimating and visualizing individual growth curves. *Structural Equation Modeling, 11,* 132–149.

Chan, D. (1998). The conceptualization and analysis of change over time: An integrative approach incorporating longitudinal mean and covariance structures analysis (LMACS) and multiple indicator latent growth modeling (MLGM). *Organizational Research Methods, 1,* 421–483.

Cheong, J., MacKinnon, D. P., & Khoo, S. T. (2003). Investigation of mediational processes using parallel process latent growth curve modeling. *Structural Equation Modeling, 10,* 238–262.

Chou, C.-P., Bentler, P. M., & Pentz, M. A. (1998). Comparisons of two statistical approaches to study growth curves: The multilevel model and the latent curve analysis. *Structural Equation Modeling, 5,* 247–266.

Cicchetti, D., & Rogosch, F. (1996). Equifinality and multifinality in developmental psychopathology. *Development and Psychopathology, 8,* 597–600.

Coffman, D. L., & Millsap, R. E. (2006). Evaluating latent growth curve models using individual fit statistics. *Structural Equation Modeling, 13,* 1–27.

Collins, L. M. (2006). Analysis of longitudinal data: The integration of theoretical model, temporal design, and statistical model. *Annual Review of Psychology, 57,* 505–528.

Cronbach, L. J., & Webb, N. (1975). Between class and within class effects in a reported aptitude × treatment interaction: A reanalysis of a study by G. L. Anderson. *Journal of Educational Psychology, 67,* 717–724.

Cudeck, R., & Klebe, K. J. (2002). Multiphase mixed-effects models for repeated measures data. *Psychological Methods, 7,* 41–63.

Curran, P. J. (2000). A latent curve framework for the study of developmental trajectories in adolescent substance use. In J. S. Rose, L. Chassin, C. C. Presson, & S. J. Sherman (Eds.), *Multivariate applications in substance use research* (pp. 1–42). Mahwah, NJ: Lawrence Erlbaum.

Curran, P. J. (2003). Have multilevel models been structural equation models all along? *Multivariate Behavioral Research, 38,* 529–569.

Curran, P. J., Bauer, D. J., & Willoughby, M. T. (2004). Testing main effects and interactions in latent curve analysis. *Psychological Methods, 9,* 220–237.

Curran, P. J., & Bollen, K. A. (2001). The best of both worlds: Combining autoregressive and latent curve models. In L. M. Collins & A. G. Sayer (Eds.), *New methods for the analysis of change* (pp. 105–136). Washington, DC: American Psychological Association.

Curran, P. J., Harford, T. C., & Muthén, B. O. (1996). The relation between heavy alcohol use and bar patronage: A latent growth model. *Journal of Studies on Alcohol, 57,* 410–418.

Curran, P. J., & Hussong, A. M. (2002). Structural equation modeling of repeated measures data. In D. Moskowitz & S. Hershberger (Eds.), *Modeling intraindividual variability with repeated measures data: Methods and applications* (pp. 59–86). New York: Lawrence Erlbaum.

Curran, P. J., & Hussong, A. M. (2003). The use of latent trajectory models in psychopathology research. *Journal of Abnormal Psychology, 112,* 526–544.

Curran, P. J., Muthén, B. O., & Harford, T. C. (1998). The influence of changes in marital status on developmental trajectories of alcohol use in young adults. *Journal of Studies on Alcohol, 59,* 647–658.

Curran, P. J., Stice, E., & Chassin, L. (1997). The relation between adolescent alcohol use and peer alcohol use: A longitudinal random coefficients model. *Journal of Consulting and Clinical Psychology, 65,* 130–140.

Curran, P. J., West, S. G., & Finch, J. F. (1996). The robustness of test statistics to nonnormality and specification error in confirmatory factor analysis. *Psychological Methods, 1,* 16–29.

Curran, P. J., & Willoughby, M. T. (2003). Implications of latent trajectory models for the study of developmental psychopathology. *Development and Psychopathology, 15,* 581–612.

de Leeuw, J., & Kreft, I. G. G. (2001). Software for multilevel analysis. In A. H. Leyland & H. Goldstein (Eds.), *Multilevel modelling of health statistics* (pp. 187–204). Chichester, UK: Wiley.

Diggle, P. J., Liang, K.-Y., & Zeger, S. L. (1994). *Analysis of longitudinal data.* Oxford, UK: Clarendon Press.

du Toit, S. H. C., & Browne, M. W. (1992). AUFIT: Automated Fitting of Non-Standard Models [Computer software].

Duncan, S. C., & Duncan, T. E. (1994). Modeling incomplete longitudinal substance use data using latent variable growth curve methodology. *Multivariate Behavioral Research, 29,* 313–338.

Duncan, S. C., & Duncan, T. E. (1996). A multivariate latent growth curve analysis of adolescent substance use. *Structural Equation Modeling, 3,* 323–347.

Duncan, S. C., Duncan, T. E., & Hops, H. (1996). Analysis of longitudinal data within accelerated longitudinal design. *Psychological Methods, 1,* 236–248.

Duncan, T. E., & Duncan, S. C. (1995). Modeling the processes of development via latent variable growth curve methodology. *Structural Equation Modeling, 2,* 187–213.

Duncan, T. E., Duncan, S. C., & Hops, H. (1993). The effects of family cohesiveness and peer encouragement on the development of adolescent alcohol use: A cohort-sequential approach to the analysis of longitudinal data. *Journal of Studies on Alcohol, 55,* 588–599.

Duncan, T. E., Duncan, S. C., & Strycker, L. A. (2006). *An introduction to latent variable growth curve modeling: Concepts, issues, and applications* (2nd ed.). Mahwah, NJ: Lawrence Erlbaum.

Duncan, T. E., Duncan, S. C., Strycker, L. A., Li, F., & Alpert, A. (1999). *An introduction to latent variable growth curve modeling: Concepts, issues, and applications.* Mahwah, NJ: Lawrence Erlbaum.

Duncan, T. E., Tildesley, E., Duncan, S. C., & Hops, H. (1995). The consistency of family and peer influences on the development of substance use in adolescence. *Addiction, 90,* 1647–1660.

Enders, C. K. (2001). A primer on maximum likelihood algorithms available for use with missing data. *Structural Equation Modeling, 8,* 128–141.

Enders, C. K., & Bandalos, D. L. (2001). The relative performance of full information maximum likelihood estimation for missing data in structural equation models. *Structural Equation Modeling, 8,* 430–457.

Ferrer, E., Hamagami, F., & McArdle, J. J. (2004). Modeling latent growth curves with incomplete data using different types of structural equation modeling and multilevel software. *Structural Equation Modeling, 11,* 452–483.

Flora, D. B., & Chassin, L. (2005). Changes in drug use during young adulthood: The effects of parent alcoholism and transition into marriage. *Psychology of Addictive Behaviors, 19,* 352–362.

Freud, A. (1958). Adolescence. In R. S. Eissler, A. Freud, H. Hartmann, & M. Kris (Eds.), *The psychoanalytic study of the child* (Vol. 13, pp. 255–278). New York: International Universities Press.

George, R. (2003). Growth in students' attitudes about the utility of science over the middle and high school years: Evidence from the Longitudinal Study of American Youth. *Journal of Science Education and Technology, 12,* 439–448.

88

Goldstein, H. (1995). *Multilevel statistical models* (2nd ed.). New York: Wiley.

Guttman, L. A. (1954). A new approach to factor analysis: The radex. In P. F. Lazarsfeld (Ed.), *Mathematical thinking in the social sciences* (pp. 258–348). New York: Columbia University Press.

Hamagami, F. (1997). A review of the Mx computer program for structural equation modeling. *Structural Equation Modeling, 4,* 157–175.

Hancock, G. R., & Choi, J. (2006). A vernacular for linear latent growth models. *Structural Equation Modeling, 13,* 352–377.

Hancock, G. R., Kuo, W.-L., & Lawrence, F. R. (2001). An illustration of second-order latent growth models. *Structural Equation Modeling, 8,* 470–489.

Hancock, G. R., & Lawrence, F. R. (2006). Using latent growth models to evaluate longitudinal change. In G. R. Hancock & R. O. Mueller (Eds.), *Structural equation modeling: A second course* (pp. 171–196). Greenwich, CT: Information Age.

Hertzog, C., Lindenberger, U., Ghisletta, P., & von Oertzen, T. (2006). On the power of multivariate latent growth curve models to detect correlated change. *Psychological Methods, 11,* 244–252.

Hofmann, D. A. (1997). An overview of the logic and rationale of hierarchical linear models. *Journal of Management, 23,* 723–744.

Hox, J. (1998). Multilevel modeling: When and why. In I. Balderjahn, R. Mathar, & M. Schader (Eds.), *Classification, data analysis, and data highways* (pp. 147–154). Berlin: Springer.

Hox, J. (2000). Multilevel analyses of grouped and longitudinal data. In T. D. Little, K. U. Schnabel, & J. Baumert (Eds.), *Modeling longitudinal and multilevel data: Practical issues, applied approaches and specific examples* (pp. 15–32). Mahwah, NJ: Lawrence Erlbaum.

Hox, J. (2002). *Multilevel analysis: Techniques and applications.* Mahwah, NJ: Lawrence Erlbaum.

Hussong, A. M., Hicks, R. E., Levy, S. A., & Curran, P. J. (2001). Specifying the relations between affect and heavy alcohol use among young adults. *Journal of Abnormal Psychology, 110,* 449–461.

Jones, B. L., Nagin, D. S., & Roeder, K. (2001). A SAS procedure based on mixture models for estimating developmental trajectories. *Sociological Methods & Research, 29,* 374–393.

Jöreskog, K. G. (1967). Some contributions to maximum likelihood factor analysis, *Psysmetrika, 32,* 443–482.

Jöreskog, K. G. (2002). *Structural equation modeling with ordinal variables using LISREL.* Retrieved January 17, 2008, from http://www.ssicentral.com

Jöreskog, K. G., & Sörbom, D. (1996). *LISREL 8 user's reference guide.* Chicago: Scientific Software International.

Khoo, S.-T., & Muthén, B. (2000). Longitudinal data on families: Growth modeling alternatives. In J. S. Rose, L. Chassin, C. C. Presson, & S. J. Sherman (Eds.), *Multivariate applications in substance use research* (pp. 43–78). Mahwah, NJ: Lawrence Erlbaum.

Kiecolt-Glaser, J. K., Glaser, R., Cacioppo, J. T., MacCallum, R. C., Snydersmith, M., Kim, C., et al. (1997). Marital conflict in older adults: Endocrinological and immunological correlates. *Psychosomatic Medicine, 59,* 350–351.

Klein, A. G., & Muthén, B. O. (2006). Modeling heterogeneity of latent growth depending on initial status. *Journal of Educational and Behavioral Statistics, 31,* 357–375.

Kline, R. B. (2004). *Principles and practice of structural equation modeling* (2nd ed.). New York: Guilford Press.

Kreft, I. G. G., & de Leeuw, J. (1998). *Introducing multilevel modeling.* London: Sage.

Lawrence, F. R., & Hancock, G. R. (1998). Assessing change over time using latent growth modeling. *Measurement and Evaluation in Counseling and Development, 30,* 211–224.

Lee, S.-Y. (2007). *Structural equation modeling: A Bayesian approach.* Hoboken, NJ: Wiley.

Lei, M., & Lomax, R. G. (2005). The effect of varying degrees of nonnormality in structural equation modeling. *Structural Equation Modeling, 12,* 1–27.

Li, F., Duncan, T. E., & Acock, A. (2000). Modeling interaction effects in latent growth curve models. *Structural Equation Modeling, 7,* 497–533.

Li, F., Duncan, T. E., Duncan, S. C., & Acock, A. (2001). Latent growth modeling of longitudinal data: A finite growth mixture modeling approach. *Structural Equation Modeling, 8,* 493–530.

Li, F., Duncan, T. E., Harmer, P., Acock, A., & Stoolmiller, M. (1998). Analyzing measurement models of latent variables through multilevel confirmatory factor analysis and hierarchical linear modeling approaches. *Structural Equation Modeling, 5,* 294–306.

Liu, H., & Powers, D. A. (2007). Growth curve models for zero-inflated count data: An application to smoking behavior. *Structural Equation Modeling, 14,* 247–279.

Longford, N. T. (1993). *Random coefficient models.* Oxford, UK: Clarendon Press.

Luke, D. A. (2004). *Multilevel modeling.* Thousand Oaks, CA: Sage.

MacCallum, R. C., Browne, M. W., & Sugawara, H. M. (1996). Power analysis and determination of sample size for covariance structure modeling. *Psychological Methods, 1,* 130–149.

MacCallum, R. C., & Kim, C. (2000). Modeling multivariate change. In T. D. Little, K. U. Schnabel, & J. Baumert (Eds.), *Modeling longitudinal and multilevel data: Practical issues, applied approaches and specific examples* (pp. 51–68). Mahwah, NJ: Lawrence Erlbaum.

MacCallum, R. C., Kim, C., Malarkey, W. B., & Kiecolt-Glaser, J. K. (1997). Studying multivariate change using multilevel models and latent curve models. *Multivariate Behavioral Research, 32,* 215–253.

MacCallum, R. C., Roznowski, M., & Necowitz, L. B. (1992). Model modification in covariance structure analysis: The problem of capitalization on chance. *Psychological Bulletin, 111,* 490–504.

Marini, M. M., Olsen, A. R., & Rubin, D. R. (1979). Maximum likelihood estimation in panel studies with missing data. In K. F. Schuessler (Ed.), *Sociological methodology 1980* (pp. 314–357). San Francisco: Jossey-Bass.

Maruyama, G. M. (1997). *Basics of structural equation modeling.* Thousand Oaks, CA: Sage.

McArdle, J. J. (1988). Dynamic but structural equation modeling of repeated measures data. In R. B. Cattell & J. Nesselroade (Eds.), *Handbook of multivariate experimental psychology* (2nd ed., pp. 561–614). New York: Plenum.

McArdle, J. J. (1989). A structural modeling experiment with multiple growth functions. In R. Kanfer, P. L. Ackerman, & R. Cudeck (Eds.), *Abilities, motivation, and methodology: The Minneapolis symposium on learning and individual differences* (pp. 71–117). Hillsdale, NJ: Lawrence Erlbaum.

McArdle, J. J. (2001). A latent difference score approach to longitudinal dynamic structural analyses. In R. Cudeck, S. du Toit, & D. Sörbom (Eds.), *Structural equation modeling: Present and future—A festschrift in honor of Karl Jöreskog* (pp. 342–380). Lincolnwood, IL: Scientific Software International.

McArdle, J. J., & Anderson, E. (1990). Latent variable growth models for research on aging. In J. E. Birren & K. W. Schaie (Eds.), *Handbook of the psychology of aging* (3rd ed., pp. 21–44). San Diego, CA: Academic Press.

McArdle, J. J., & Bell, R. Q. (2000). An introduction to latent growth models for developmental data analysis. In T. D. Little, K. U. Schnabel, & J. Baumert (Eds.), *Modeling longitudinal and multilevel data: Practical issues, applied approaches and specific examples.* Mahwah, NJ: Lawrence Erlbaum.

McArdle, J. J., & Epstein, D. (1987). Latent growth curves within developmental structural equation models. *Child Development, 58,* 110–133.

McArdle, J. J., & Hamagami, F. (1991). Modeling incomplete longitudinal data using latent growth structural equation models. In L. Collins & J. L. Horn (Eds.), *Best methods for the analysis of change* (pp. 276–304). Washington, DC: American Psychological Association.

McArdle, J. J., & Hamagami, F. (1992). Modeling incomplete longitudinal and cross-sectional data using latent growth structural models. *Experimental Aging Research, 18,* 145–166.

McArdle, J. J., & Hamagami, F. (2001). Latent difference score structural models for linear dynamic analyses with incomplete longitudinal data. In L. M. Collins & A. G. Sayer (Eds.), *New methods for the analysis of change* (pp. 139–175). Washington, DC: American Psychological Association.

Mehta, P. D., & Neale, M. C. (2005). People are variables too: Multilevel structural equation modeling. *Psychological Methods, 10,* 259–284.

Mehta, P. D., Neale, M. C., & Flay, B. R. (2004). Squeezing interval change from ordinal panel data: Latent growth curves with ordinal outcomes. *Psychological Methods, 9,* 301–333.

Mehta, P. D., & West, S. G. (2000). Putting the individual back into individual growth curves. *Psychological Methods, 5,* 23–43.

Meredith, W., & Horn, J. (2001). The role of factorial invariance in modeling growth and change. In L. M. Collins & A. G. Sayer (Eds.), *New methods for the analysis of change* (pp. 201–240). Washington, DC: American Psychological Association.

Meredith, W., & Tisak, J. (1990). Latent curve analysis. *Psychometrika, 55,* 107–122.

Miller, B. C., Benson, B., & Galbraith, K. A. (2001). Family relationship and adolescent pregnancy risk: A research synthesis. *Developmental Review, 21,* 1–38.

Miyazaki, Y., & Raudenbush, S. W. (2000). Tests for linkage of multiple cohorts in an accelerated longitudinal design. *Psychological Methods, 5,* 44–63.

Muthén, B. (1993). Latent variable modeling of growth with missing data and multilevel data. In C. M. Cuadras & C. R. Rao (Eds.), *Multivariate analysis: Future directions 2* (pp. 199–210). Amsterdam: North Holland.

Muthén, B. (1997). Latent variable modeling of longitudinal and multilevel data. In A. Raftery (Ed.), *Sociological methodology* (pp. 453–480). Boston: Blackwell.

Muthén, B. (2000). Methodological issues in random coefficient growth modeling using a latent variable framework: Applications to the development of heavy drinking ages 18–37. In J. S. Rose, L. Chassin, C. C. Presson, & S. J. Sherman (Eds.), *Multivariate applications in substance use research* (pp. 113–140). Mahwah, NJ: Lawrence Erlbaum.

Muthén, B. (2001). Latent variable mixture modeling. In G. A. Marcoulides & R. E. Schumacker (Eds.), *New developments and techniques in structural equation modeling* (pp. 1–33). Mahwah, NJ: Lawrence Erlbaum.

Muthén, B., & Asparouhov, T. (2002). Latent variable analysis with categorical outcomes: Multiple-group and growth modeling in Mplus. *Mplus Web Note: No. 4.* Retrieved January 17, 2008, from http://www.statmodel.com/download/webnotes/CatMGLong.pdf

Muthén, B., Kaplan, D., & Hollis, M. (1987). On structural equation modeling with data that are not missing completely at random. *Psychometrika, 52,* 431–462.

Muthén, B. O., & Curran, P. J. (1997). General longitudinal modeling of individual differences in experimental designs: A latent variable framework for analysis and power estimation. *Psychological Methods, 2,* 371–402.

Muthén, L. K., & Muthén, B. O. (1998–2006). *Mplus user's guide.* Los Angeles: Muthén & Muthén.

Nagin, D. (1999). Analyzing developmental trajectories: A semi-parametric, group-based approach. *Psychological Methods, 4,* 139–177.

Nagin, D., & Tremblay, R. E. (2001). Analyzing developmental trajectories of distinct but related behaviors: A group-based method. *Psychological Methods, 6,* 18–34.

Neale, M. C. (2000). Individual fit, heterogeneity, and missing data in multigroup structural equation modeling. In T. D. Little, K. U. Schnabel, & J. Baumert (Eds.), *Modeling longitudinal and multilevel data: Practical issues, applied approaches and specific examples* (pp. 249–267). Mahwah, NJ: Lawrence Erlbaum.

Neale, M. C., Boker, S. M., Xie, G., & Maes, H. H. (2003). *Mx: Statistical modeling* (6th ed.). Richmond, VA: Department of Psychiatry, Virginia Commonwealth University.

Neale, M. C., & Miller, M. B. (1997). The use of likelihood-based confidence intervals in genetic models. *Behavior Genetics, 27,* 113–120.

Nesselroade, J. R., & Baltes, P. B. (1979). *Longitudinal research in the study of behavior and development.* New York: Academic Press.

NICHD Early Child Care Research Network. (2006). Child-care effect sizes for the NICHD study of early child care and youth development. *American Psychologist, 61,* 99–116.

Pianta, R. C. (1993). *The Student–Teacher Relationship Scale.* Charlottesville: University of Virginia Press.

Potthoff, R. F., & Roy, S. N. (1964). A generalized multivariate analysis of variance model useful especially for growth curve problems. *Biometrika, 51,* 313–326.

Preacher, K. J., Curran, P. J., & Bauer, D. J. (2006). Computational tools for probing interaction effects in multiple linear regression, multilevel modeling, and latent curve analysis. *Journal of Educational and Behavioral Statistics, 31,* 437–448.

Rao, C. R. (1958). Some statistical models for comparison of growth curves. *Biometrics, 14,* 1–17.

Rasbash, J., Browne, W., Goldstein, H., Yang, M., Plewis, I., Healy, M., et al. (1999). *A user's guide to MLwiN.* London: Multilevel Models Project.

Raudenbush, S. W. (2001). Toward a coherent framework for comparing trajectories of individual change. In L. M. Collins and A. G. Sayers (Eds.), *New methods for the analysis of change* (pp. 33–64). Washington, DC: American Psychological Association.

Raudenbush, S. W., Brennan, R. T., & Barnett, R. C. (1995). A multivariate hierarchical model for studying psychological change within married couples. *Journal of Family Psychology, 9,* 161–176.

Raudenbush, S. W., & Bryk, A. S. (2002). *Hierarchical linear models: Applications and data analysis methods* (2nd ed.). Thousand Oaks, CA: Sage.

Raudenbush, S. W., & Chan, W. (1992). Growth curve analysis in accelerated longitudinal designs. *Journal of Research in Crime and Delinquency, 29,* 387–411.

Raudenbush, S. W., & Chan, W.-S. (1993). Application of a hierarchical linear model to the study of adolescent deviance in an overlapping cohort design. *Journal of Consulting and Clinical Psychology, 61,* 941–951.

Raykov, T., & Marcoulides, G. A. (2000). *A first course in structural equation modeling.* Hillsdale, NJ: Lawrence Erlbaum.

Rodebaugh, T. L., Curran, P. J., & Chambless, D. L. (2002). Expectancy of panic in the maintenance of daily anxiety in panic disorder with agoraphobia: A longitudinal test of competing models. *Behavior Therapy, 33,* 315–336.

Rogosa, D. R., & Willett, J. B. (1985). Understanding correlates of change by modeling individual differences in growth. *Psychometrika, 50,* 203–228.

Rovine, M. J., & Molenaar, P. C. M. (2000). A structural modeling approach to a multilevel random coefficients model. *Multivariate Behavioral Research, 35,* 51–88.

Rubin, D. B. (1976). Inference and missing data. *Biometrika, 63,* 581–592.

Sayer, A. G., & Cumsille, P. E. (2001). Second-order latent growth models. In L. M. Collins & A. G. Sayer (Eds.), *New methods for the analysis of change* (pp. 179–200). Washington, DC: American Psychological Association.

92

Sayer, A. G., & Willett, J. B. (1998). A cross-domain model for growth in adolescent expectancies. *Multivariate Behavioral Research, 33,* 509–543.

Schaie, K. W. (1965). A general model for the study of developmental problems. *Psychological Bulletin, 64,* 92–107.

Schaie, K. W. (1986). Beyond calendar definitions of age, time, and cohort: The general developmental model revisited. *Developmental Review, 6,* 252–277.

Scheines, R., Hoijtink, H., & Boomsma, A. (1999). Bayesian estimation and testing of structural equation models. *Psychometrika, 64,* 37–52.

Simons-Morton, B. G., Chen, R., Abroms, R., & Haynie, D. L. (2004). Latent growth curve analyses of peer and parent influences on smoking stage progression among early adolescents. *Health Psychology, 23,* 612–621.

Singer, J. D., & Willett, J. B. (2003). *Applied longitudinal data analysis: Modeling change and event occurrence.* New York: Oxford University Press.

Smetana, J. G. (1988). Concepts of self and social convention: Adolescents' and parents' reasoning about hypothetical and actual family conflicts. In M. R. Gunnar & W. A. Collins (Eds.), *The Minnesota Symposia on Child Psychology: Vol. 21. Development during the transition to adolescence* (pp. 43–77). Hillsdale, NJ: Lawrence Erlbaum.

Snijders, T., & Bosker, R. (1999). *Multilevel analysis: An introduction to basic and advanced multilevel modeling.* London: Sage.

Stack, S., & Eshleman, J. R. (1998). Marital status and happiness: A 17-nation study. *Journal of Marriage and the Family, 60,* 527–536.

Steiger, J. H., & Lind, J. M. (1980, June). *Statistically based tests for the number of common factors.* Paper presented at the annual meeting of the Psychometric Society, Iowa City, IA.

Steinberg, L. (1989). Pubertal maturation and parent-adolescent distance: An evolutionary perspective. In G. Adams, R. Montemayor, & T. Gullotta (Eds.), *Biology of adolescent behavior and development* (pp. 82–114). Newbury Park, CA: Sage.

Sterba, S., Prinstein, M. J., & Cox, M. J. (2007). Trajectories of internalizing problems across childhood: Heterogeneity, external validity, and gender differences. *Development and Psychopathology, 19,* 345–366.

Stoel, R. D. (2003). *Issues in growth curve modeling.* Unpublished doctoral dissertation, University of Amsterdam, The Netherlands.

Stoel, R. D., & van den Wittenboer, G. (2003). Time dependence of growth parameters in latent growth curve models with time invariant covariates. *Methods of Psychological Research Online, 8,* 21–41.

Stoel, R. D., van den Wittenboer, G., & Hox, J. (2004). Including time-invariant covariates in the latent growth curve model. *Structural Equation Modeling, 11,* 155–167.

Stoolmiller, M. (1995). Using latent growth curve models to study developmental processes. In J. M. Gottman (Ed.), *The analysis of change* (pp. 103–138). Mahwah, NJ: Lawrence Erlbaum.

Tisak, J., & Meredith, W. (1989). Exploratory longitudinal factor analysis in multiple populations. *Psychometrika, 54,* 261–281.

Tisak, J., & Meredith, W. (1990). Descriptive and associative developmental models. In A. von Eye (Ed.), *Statistical methods in longitudinal research* (Vol. 2, pp. 387–406). Boston: Academic Press.

Tisak, J., & Tisak, M. S. (1996). Longitudinal models of reliability and validity: A latent curve approach. *Applied Psychological Measurement, 20,* 275–288.

Tisak, J., & Tisak, M. S. (2000). Permanency and ephemerality of psychological measures with application to organizational commitment. *Psychological Methods, 5,* 175–198.

Tonry, M., Ohlin, L. E., & Farrington, D. P. (1991). *Human development and criminal behavior: New ways of advancing knowledge.* New York: Springer-Verlag.

Tucker, L. R (1958). Determination of parameters of a functional relation by factor analysis. *Psychometrika, 23,* 19–23.

Tucker, L. R (1966). Learning theory and multivariate experiment: Illustration by determination of parameters of generalized learning curves. In R. B. Cattell (Ed.), *Handbook of multivariate experimental psychology* (pp. 476–501). Chicago: Rand McNally.

Tucker, L. R, & Lewis, C. (1973). A reliability coefficient for maximum likelihood factor analysis. *Psychometrika, 38,* 1–10.

VanLaningham, J., Johnson, D. R., & Amato, P. (2001). Marital happiness, marital duration, and the U-shaped curve: Evidence from a five-wave panel study. *Social Forces, 78,* 1313–1341.

von Eye, A., & Bergman, L. R. (2003). Research strategies in developmental psychopathology: Dimensional identity and the person-oriented approach. *Development and Psychopathology, 15,* 553–580.

Wang, J. (2004). Significance testing for outcome changes via latent growth model. *Structural Equation Modeling, 11,* 375–400.

Wang, M., & Bodner, T. E. (2007). Growth mixture modeling: Identifying and predicting unobserved subpopulations with longitudinal data. *Organizational Research Methods, 10,* 635–656.

Wendorf, C. A. (2002). Comparisons of structural equation modeling and hierarchical linear modeling approaches to couples' data. *Structural Equation Modeling, 9,* 126–140.

Widaman, K. F., & Thompson, J. S. (2003). On specifying the null model for incremental fit indices in structural equation modeling. *Psychological Methods, 8,* 16–37.

Willett, J. B. (1989). Questions and answers in the measurement of change. In E. Z. Rothkopf (Ed.), *Review of research in education* (Vol. 15, pp. 345–422). Washington, DC: American Education Research Association.

Willett, J. B., & Sayer, A. G. (1994). Using covariance structure analysis to detect correlates and predictors of individual change over time. *Psychological Bulletin, 116,* 363–381.

Willett, J. B., & Sayer, A. G. (1995). Cross-domain analyses of change over time: Combining growth modeling and covariance structure analysis. In G. A. Marcoulides & R. E. Schumacker (Eds.), *Advanced structural equation modeling: Issues and techniques* (pp. 125–157). Mahwah, NJ: Lawrence Erlbaum.

Willett, J. B., Singer, J. D., & Martin, N. C. (1998). The design and analysis of longitudinal studies of development and psychopathology in context: Statistical models and methodological recommendations. *Development and Psychopathology, 10,* 395–426.

Wills, T. A., Cleary, S. D., Filer, M., Shinar, O., Mariani, J., & Spera, K. (2001). Temperament related to early-onset substance use: Test of a developmental model. *Prevention Science, 2,* 145–163.

Wothke, W. (2000). Longitudinal and multigroup modeling with missing data. In T. D. Little, K. U. Schnabel, & J. Baumert (Eds.), *Modeling longitudinal and multilevel data: Practical issues, applied approaches and specific examples* (pp. 219–240). Mahwah, NJ: Lawrence Erlbaum.

Zhang, Z., Hamagami, F., Wang, L., Nesselroade, J. R., & Grimm, K. J. (2007). Bayesian analysis of longitudinal data using growth curve models. *International Journal of Behavioral Development, 31,* 374–383.

INDEX

Accelerated longitudinal design, 42
Analysis of covariance (ANCOVA), 5
Aperture, 33, 56 (n7)
Aspects of change, 4
Assumptions, 14–15
Autoregressive latent trajectory
    model, 15, 66, 70

Bayesian method, 80–81

Change point, 60
Chi-square, 18–20
Child-Parent Relationship Scale, 22
Close fit, test of, 20
Cohort-sequential design, 42–46, 70
Confidence interval, likelihood-based,
    50, 56 (n11)
Covariance structure, 6

Data model, 6
Definition variable, 14, 47–50
Degrees of freedom, 12, 18, 21 (n9)
Deviance statistic, 75
Discontinuity design, 59
Disturbance, 6, 80
    variance, 8, 10, 21 (n4), 26, 30–31,
        55 (n3), 61–62
Dynamic consistency, 62

Empirical Bayes estimate, 76
Exact fit, test of, 20
Exploratory factor analysis, 4

Factor
    first-order, 62
    second-order, 62
    shape, 52–53
    unique, 63 (note)

Factor covariance, 7–8, 10–11, 28,
    31–33
Factor loading, 6–8, 10–11, 13–14, 25,
    28, 44, 59–62, 64–65
Factor mean, 7–8, 10, 26, 28, 60–61
Factor score, 76–77
Factor variance, 7–8, 10–11, 26, 28,
    30–31, 33
Factorial invariance, longitudinal, 62
Fixed coefficient, 72

Growth mixture model, 57–59, 80

Individual data vector, 14
Interaction, 70, 80
    cross-level, 36, 56 (n9), 82
    intercept by treatment, 68
    plotting, 82
Intercept, 7, 10
    fixed, 28, 72
    random, 26–28, 30–33, 72–74
    variance, 26, 30, 31, 33, 73
Intercept factor, 6
Intraclass correlation (ICC), 30

Knot, 60

Latent curve analysis, 5
Latent growth mixture modeling
    (LGMM), 57–59, 80
Latent growth curve modeling
    assumptions of, 14–15
    differences from multilevel
        modeling, 77–79
    flexibility of, 5
    history of, 4–5
    overlap with multilevel modeling,
        75–77

Likelihood ratio test, 20
Longitudinal factor analysis, 81

Maximum likelihood, 15–18, 74
  assumptions of, 15
  full information (FIML), 17–18,
    44, 46, 74, 79
  restricted (REML), 74, 79
Mean structure, 6
Method of convergence, 42
Missing data, 16–18, 21 (n6, n7),
  43–44, 46, 72, 79
Model
  associative latent growth
    curve, 39
  autoregressive, 66
  autoregressive latent trajectory
    (ALT), 66, 70
  bivariate growth, 39
  completely latent, 53
  conditional latent growth curve,
    35–38
  cross-domain individual
    growth, 39
  curve-of-factors, 62
  fixed intercept, fixed slope, 28–30
  fully latent, 53
  fully multivariate latent trajectory, 39
  growth mixture, 57–59, 80
  hierarchical linear, 71
  latent difference score, 66
  latent growth mixture (LGMM),
    57–59, 80
  latent variable longitudinal
    curve, 62
  linear latent growth curve,
    9 (figure)
  Markov simplex, 66
  mixed, 71
  multilevel (see Multilevel
    modeling)
  multiphase, 60

  multiple-domain, 39
  multiple-groups, 34–35, 70
  multivariate change, 39
  nested, 19, 53, 55 (n5)
  null, 25–26
  parallel process, 38–42, 70
  piecewise growth, 59, 70
  polynomial latent growth
    curve, 50–52
  quadratic latent growth curve,
    50–52
  random coefficient, 71
  random intercept, 26–28
  random intercept, fixed slope,
    30–31
  random intercept, random slope,
    31–33
  second-order latent growth, 62
  simultaneous growth, 39
  structured latent curve (SLC),
    62–65
  unconditional latent growth
    curve, 36
  unspecified trajectory, 52–53
  variance component, 71
Model evaluation, 18–20
Model fit indices, 18–20
Model modification, 78
Model selection, 18–20
Multilevel modeling, 61, 70, 71–79
  differences from latent growth
    curve modeling, 77–79
  estimation, 74
  evaluation, 75
  flexibility of, 72
  overlap with latent growth curve
    modeling, 75–77
  specification of, 73–74
Multilevel structural equation model,
  77–78
Multiple-groups analysis, 34–35,
  42–43, 46

National Institute of Child Health and
    Human Development, 22–23
Nested data, 71
Non-normed fit index (NNFI), 19, 44
Nonlinearity, 50–52, 62–65

Path diagram, 9, 27, 29, 37, 40, 45,
    47, 49, 51, 54, 63, 67, 69
Period, 60
Polynomial trend, 50–52
Posterior mean, 76
Power, 20
Principal components analysis, 4

Random coefficient, 7, 72
Random effect, 7
Random-effects ANOVA, 72
Regime, 60
Repeated measures, number of, 12
Root mean square error of
    approximation (RMSEA), 18–20

Sample size, 20
SEM (see Structural equation
    modeling)
Shape factor, 52–53
Shrinkage estimate, 76
Slope, 29
    fixed, 28, 30–31, 72
    random, 31–33, 72–74
    variance, 31, 33, 73
Slope factor, 6
Software
    aML, 79
    AMOS, 3, 17, 23
    AUFIT, 65
    EQS, 3, 17, 23, 79
    GAUSS, 59
    HLM, 74, 79
    LISREL, 3, 17–18, 21 (n2), 23,
        54 (n2), 65, 67, 79, 83

MIX, 79
MLwiN, 74, 76, 79
Mplus, 3, 17, 21 (n7), 23, 54 (n2),
    59, 67, 77, 79, 83
Multilevel, 79
Mx, 3, 17, 23, 54 (n2), 59, 67, 83
OLStraj, 82–83
R, 79
SAS, 59, 79
Splus, 79
SPSS, 79
Stata, 79
SYSTAT, 79
Standardized root mean square
    residual (SRMR), 19
Stationarity, 62
Structural equation modeling, 3, 5
    multilevel, 77–78
Structured latent curve (SLC),
    52, 62–65
Student-Teacher Relationship Scale, 22

Target function, 64
Theory, role of, 18, 54
Time, scaling of, 10–14
Time-invariant covariate, 25,
    35–38, 74
Time-varying covariate (TVC), 24–25,
    46–50, 70, 74
Trajectory, 2
Treatment effect, 68–69

Variables
    categorical, 66–68
    latent, 6, 61–62
    measured, 6
    ordinal, 66–68
Variance
    common, 61
    error, 61–62
    unique, 61

WITHDRAWN FROM
JUNIATA COLLEGE LIBRARY